The Power of

DESIGN FOR σ SIX SIGMA

OTHER BOOKS BY SUBIR CHOWDHURY

The Power of Six Sigma: An Inspiring Tale of How Six Sigma Is Transforming the Way We Work

Robust Engineering: Learn How to Boost Quality While Reducing Costs & Time to Market

Design for Six Sigma: The Revolutionary Process for Achieving Extraordinary Profits

The Talent Era: Achieving a High Return on Talent

Management 21C: Someday We'll All Manage This Way

Organization 21C: Someday All Organizations Will Lead This Way

QS-9000 Pioneers: Registered Companies Share Their Strategies for Success

The Mahalanobis-Taguchi System

The Power of

DESIGN FOR σ SIX SIGMA

Subir Chowdhury

Dearborn™
Trade Publishing
A **Kaplan Professional** Company

This publication is designed to provide accurate and authoritative information in regard to the subject matter covered. It is sold with the understanding that the publisher is not engaged in rendering legal, accounting, or other professional service. If legal advice or other expert assistance is required, the services of a competent professional should be sought.

Vice President and Publisher: Cynthia A. Zigmund
Editorial Director: Donald J. Hull
Senior Acquisitions Editor: Jean Iversen
Senior Managing Editor: Jack Kiburz
Interior Design: Lucy Jenkins
Cover Design: Scott Rattray, Rattray Design
Typesetting: Elizabeth Pitts

Robust Design® is a registered trademark of ASI–American Supplier Institute.

Published by Dearborn Trade Publishing
A Kaplan Professional Company

Printed in the United States of America

03 04 05 10 9 8 7 6 5 4 3 2 1

Library of Congress Cataloging-in-Publication Data

Chowdhury, Subir.
  The power of design for Six Sigma / Subir Chowdhury.
    p. cm.
  ISBN 0-7931-6060-X (hardcover)
  1. Industrial management. I. Title.
HD31 .C5138 2002
658—dc21   2002011319

Dearborn Trade books are available at special quantity discounts to use as premiums and sales promotions, or for use in corporate training programs. For more information, please call the Special Sales Manager at 800-621-9621, ext. 4410, or e-mail Mindi Rowland at rowland@dearborn.com.

PRAISE FOR THE POWER OF DESIGN FOR SIX SIGMA

"Chowdhury has done it again. He's simplified the concepts of Design for Six Sigma (DFSS) and given us all an indispensable tool to use when communicating DFSS to the masses. His fresh approach makes DFSS interesting—speaking to a common denominator and establishing a foundation on which to build in-depth knowledge of DFSS and its application in healthcare."

    —Peter McCabe, General Manager
    GE Medical Systems Six Sigma for Healthcare™

"Subir Chowdhury continues to take the mystery out of what seems to be a complex concept. This book offers powerful insight into the importance of designing a process right the first time. The clarity of how Design for Six Sigma (DFSS) can be applied in a service industry will energize you to explore process design in a way that will delight your customers and bring measurable results to your company."

    —Joseph T. Calvaruso, President and
    Chief Executive Officer
    Mount Carmel Health System

"Subir's new book, *The Power of Design for Six Sigma,* offers great insight into a major breakthrough opportunity. Using Six Sigma tools in the product development process will achieve design for quality, design for manufacturability,

design for costs, and design for customer service. This book highlights the way to do things right the first time."
—Timothy C. Tyson, President,
   Global Manufacturing & Supply
   GlaxoSmithKline

"In *The Power of Design for Six Sigma,* Subir Chowdhury conveys the power of DFSS in an approachable, enjoyable style. The book is a great introduction to one of the most relevant and impactful management tools of our time."
—Mike Allan, Vice President–Six Sigma
   Black&Decker, Inc.

DEDICATION

To the memory of my very dear friend
PHILIP B. CROSBY

CONTENTS

PREFACE

In the summer of 2001, I introduced Joe Meter as the central character in my book, *The Power of Six Sigma*. At the beginning of the book, we saw Joe hit rock bottom when he was asked to pack up all his belongings in a cardboard box and leave the company he had served faithfully for years. By the end of the book, Joe had been reenergized by his lunch with Larry Hogan—but I never did reveal whether or not Joe got another job.

Since then, I have received thousands of e-mails and letters from my readers all over the world—from Argentina to Australia, India to Italy, and the United Kingdom to the United States—to find out what happened to Joe. This showed me something. People really do care about people, regardless of race or religion, or whether they're coworkers or customers.

Although Six Sigma and Design for Six Sigma (DFSS) are business strategies, they still boil down to trusting basic human nature—that we really do care about each other, and that we understand we have to work together to move ahead. Both Six Sigma and DFSS depend on the combination of process power with people power, without which neither will succeed.

In this book, *The Power of Design for Six Sigma,* I reveal the secrets of Joe's comeback. Joe transformed himself from a stuck-in-the-mud middle manager into a highly successful and innovative business professional by understanding and caring about the customer.

The book you are holding in your hands I created for the customers. Yes, the CUSTOMERS—the KING and QUEEN! I don't necessarily expect customers to read this book, but I do expect the wisdom herein to help them get what they want out of business. Along these lines, I have emphasized the importance of understanding the true voice of the customer. Most of us note these vital voices but do not translate them into products and services that create customer excitement. The more you care about people—especially your customers—the more you win.

Effective communication at all levels is the key if any major organizational initiative is going to succeed. If companies do not effectively communicate the Six Sigma or DFSS philosophies, they will not get results. I felt my mission with *The Power of Six Sigma* was fulfilled when I saw organizations around the world using it to communicate this philosophy to their employees.

The vast majority of organizations have had great success implementing Six Sigma, but when they struggle, I have found, it's usually because the company's CEO or executive leaders feel that Six Sigma is the sole domain of technical people—a major misconception. Most also feel that they must implement Six Sigma before adopting DFSS—another misconception. This book seeks to dispel those myths by demonstrating that organizations can deploy both processes simultaneously.

This is a book about achieving perfection. It stresses the importance of Voice of the Customer and a process called Robust Optimization—two vital methodologies that are rarely practiced correctly by most organizations. Even most so-called expert consultants do not teach these correctly. I've written this book to help ensure that the message is clear and easy to follow. I've written it to help middle managers charged with pursuing this philosophy, customers who will benefit from it, and CEOs who write huge checks to consulting firms without knowing what DFSS really is or how it works. But most of all, I've written it for the "rest of us"—the line workers, the engineers, the support staff, and all the others in nonmanagerial positions who fear yet another program coming down the pike and what it might mean to them and their jobs. This book will help them all and, in the process, help their companies achieve the lofty goals only DFSS can achieve.

My hope is that *The Power of Design for Six Sigma* will simplify what can be a complicated, intimidating subject in a lively, entertaining style—the way its predecessor *The Power of Six Sigma* did—and make DFSS easily understandable by all. My mission will be complete with this book if it helps people around the globe focus on preventing crises and understanding the customer in everything they do.

Subir Chowdhury
Executive Vice President, ASI–American Supplier Institute
E-mail: subir.chowdhury@asiusa.com
Web site: <www.asiusa.com>

FEELING FLAT

I woke up this morning feeling flat. No motivation to wake up. No desire to go to the office. Feeling like I should be doing something else—anything else.

On the surface, there was nothing wrong, really. My wife and kids were fine, and I was still a vice president at American Foods, heading up the American Pizza division—but nothing felt really right. I was tired of my job and, as a result, bored and uninspired by my life. Waking up and starting my day, I suddenly realized, had become a chore. If I was going to keep going, something was going to have to give. Was it time to quit? Find another job? Even retire from business to pursue something else entirely? I had no answers, and I was surprised to find myself entertaining such wild ideas—ideas I'd never have considered just a few weeks ago.

When I got the top job at American Pizza five years ago, after 15 years working my way up from the mail room at American Burger, I was full of spit and vinegar. I had a million ideas, a bunch of big dreams, and more energy to pursue them all than any one man should be allowed.

My biggest idea, though, wasn't my idea at all—in business, it doesn't have to be. Steal from the best, I say, and make it your own. I decided early on that my division would follow the principles of Six Sigma, a scientific, customer-based approach to corporate improvement. It worked. In a short period of time, we woke up a moribund franchise and turned it into a gleaming example of business at its best. We increased profits dramatically—mainly by cutting costs—all the while cranking up our customer satisfaction ratings and reducing our employee turnover to a trickle.

We were heroes, on the cover of just about every business publication and even *Time* magazine. "The Pizza Barons," the *Time* cover said, "Larry Hogan & Co. Set the Standard and Leave the Rest Behind." It was about as good as it gets, a thrilling period when everything seemed new, and the possibilities seemed limitless.

Well, three years later, we're still making good profits, keeping our customers and employees happy, and generally running a good business. But when I woke up this morning, a bunch of nagging thoughts crystallized into one depressing conclusion: We're not one bit better today than we were three years ago.

Okay, I grant you that there's something to be said simply for maintaining a great organization and not making the kinds of mistakes that can ruin a good thing. But when I look at our numbers—for revenues, for profits, for the Customer Satisfaction Index (CSI), and the like—they're really not one notch better. And that concerns me. That bothers me.

How did we climb so far so fast, only to stall for three years? And how do we get out of this rut? That's the thought that hit me like a ton of bricks as I sat there on the edge of the bed, dreading the start of another day of more of the same. I felt like the guy in the donut commercial, getting up in an almost hypnotic trance, saying over and over again, "It's time to make the donuts. " I felt like my work had been reduced to making endless batches of donuts, every day.

I dragged myself to the shower, to the closet, to the breakfast table. I slogged to the car with my cup of coffee and got on the road. I actually started thinking that this might be my last day at this job. In fact, like sneezing, once the idea entered my mind, I couldn't get rid of it. It took me by surprise and dominated my thinking. "This might be the day I quit my job." I decided that was it—unless something fell out of the sky to change my mind, I was going to submit my resignation today. I suddenly felt light and relieved. It was the only thought that gave me any relief from the idea of returning to the mind-numbing tedium of my work.

I flipped around a few radio stations and listened to the same old morning deejays yacking away, when I heard a familiar voice.

"What we wanted to do, Jim, is not just open another coffee shop, but really reinvent the whole coffee experience," the radio guest said.

I banged the steering wheel and yelled, "That's Joe!" Then I realized I was talking to no one and chuckled at myself. I'll be! I thought. Joe Meter, my old friend from the American Burger mail room two decades ago. The same guy who had gotten fired five years ago from American Burger and was lower than a snake's belly when he called me for lunch the same day they'd let him go. After 15 years at the same company, they made him clean out his desk with a security guard watching over him.

Six Sigma Simplified

Some lunch! By the end of my explanation of Six Sigma, Joe's whole outlook on business—and his future—had been transformed. I won't bore you with all the details, because you might have a working knowledge of it already. So, in a nutshell, Six Sigma is a management philosophy that focuses on eliminating mistakes, waste, and rework. Where most programs focus on "offense"—that is, making more products, increasing volume, developing whiz-bang marketing concepts—Six Sigma focuses on "defense," on doing many of the things you're already doing but doing them better and with fewer mistakes.

But I want to be clear about this: Six Sigma is not a rah-rah "Do Better" program; it's a measurable status to strive for, a strategic problem-solving method to increase customer satisfaction and dramatically enhance the bottom line. Six Sigma teaches your employees how to improve the way they do business, scientifically and fundamentally, and maintain their new performance level for years.

Before I continue I should explain—if you don't know already—that *Sigma* is a Greek letter that indicates the capability of any given process to perform defect-free work. The higher the Sigma value, the fewer defects you have—Six Sigma being virtually perfect. One Sigma, for example, means you're making about 700,000 defects per million opportunities, or DPMO, a 30 percent success rate—clearly unacceptable for anyone who doesn't play left field for the Yankees. If you're working at Two Sigma, you're making a little over 300,000 mistakes per million opportunities, or a 70 percent batting average.

Most companies operate between Three and Four Sigma, which means they make between approximately 67,000 and 6,000 mistakes per million chances. Operating at 3.8 Sigma means that you're getting it right 99 percent of the time. To most people, that sounds like virtual perfection, when actually, a 99 percent success rate is the equivalent of 20,000 lost articles of mail every hour, 5,000 botched surgical procedures every week, or four accidents per day at major airports. These are levels of failure the American public would never accept, and rightly so. The goal, therefore, is to go higher—as high as Six Sigma, if possible.

As I told Joe that eventful day, Six Sigma gives you discipline, structure, and a foundation for solid decision making based on simple statistics. It also maximizes your return on investment and your Return on Talent™—your people.

Joe Gets a Job

When I first told Joe about Six Sigma, he almost groaned; he'd been through so many business initiatives. He was skeptical, to say the least. But by the end of our lunch, he was sold. It's no exaggeration to say that Six Sigma completely changed Joe's career path. He'd even tell you it changed his life.

He left the restaurant that day with a bounce in his step. His future was still uncertain, of course, and he still had to tell his family the bad news about being fired, but he said he felt he was onto something and that everything would work out. Although it took some doing—and some old-fashioned elbow grease— it's fair to say everything has worked out for Joe, better than anyone really could have expected.

Instead of just beating the pavement, Joe actually researched the companies he wanted to work for—a pretty bold move, since beggars can't be choosers. He wanted more than a job, he said. He wanted to work for a company where he could thrive. That way, he figured, he'd be excited about his future prospects, and the company would be excited about hiring him.

Joe took his time looking, but it worked. He impressed the four companies who interviewed him as an eager, confident, and forward-thinking man. Joe had something the other candidates didn't have: a vision. And that's pretty rare for guys who don't have jobs! Joe received three offers and was mulling them over when I gave him a call.

I told him about a position at my shop, American Pizza, that had just opened up. It was a couple levels below me, it paid a little less than two of his three offers, but Joe took the job. And, thanks to the other offers he already had, I could justify to my bosses why I was hiring a guy that American Burger had just fired!

He worked hard, and he worked well, moving up the ranks, saving the company lots of money through Six Sigma—and helping me look good! I gave him lots of accountability but also the autonomy necessary to get the job done without constantly being second-guessed. Perhaps most important, I wanted him to succeed—partly because of our old friendship but also, I think, because Six Sigma is set up to recognize managers for the progress of their employees. Joe once told me he learned more about management by working for two years at American Pizza than he had for 15 years at American Burger.

Joe was happy, his wife was happy, his kids were happy. He was probably in the best position of his life. And, he felt like he was making an important contribution to the team—something everyone needs to feel.

Looking at the future, we both figured I would get promoted to the upper floors of the parent company, American Foods, giving Joe the opportunity to take my place at the top of American Pizza.

But that's not the way things worked out. As John Lennon once said, "Life is what happens when you're making other plans."

Joe's New Job

While Joe was still working for me at American Pizza, he and his family took a vacation in Italy. His wife had wanted to go there for some time to visit relatives in Florence, but they waited until the kids were old enough to enjoy the trip. The kids, of course, loved the canals and the beaches and the Italian ices. Joe's wife, Kelly, loved the museums and the shopping. But what caught Joe's fancy were the cafés on every corner. Yes, the cafés. I've never been to Italy, but from what Joe told me, the Italian approach to coffee is entirely different from ours.

It's hard to remember now, but just a few years ago we Americans were content to slurp down whatever swill was being spat out at the local fast-food joint or donut shop, or even the gas station mini-mart on the way to work. Nothing special about the coffee or the experience, that's for sure. It had all the romance of pumping gas down your gullet.

It struck Joe that the Italians happily spent two and three times more money than we did for much better coffee—better beans, more flavor, more varieties. They also slowed down to enjoy it at beautiful intimate cafés where no one rushed them to get out and leave their table for the next customer. They were allowed to sit and enjoy themselves, by reading the paper, chatting with friends, or just relaxing. Joe started going to these cafés every day while his wife shopped, and by the end of his vacation, he was hooked.

Well, as luck would have it, shortly after Joe returned home the bigwigs at American Foods decided it was time to venture into the coffee market by opening a new division called American Coffee. They figured they were already paying big bucks to outside vendors to supply the American Pizza and American

Burger stores with coffee, so why not do it in-house and keep the profits?

Why not, indeed! Naturally, they needed managers to run the operation, so they started asking their top executives for candidates. I recommended Joe, though I added that I'd hate to lose him. Long story short, when they saw Joe's unexpected passion for the Italian cafés—and Six Sigma—they offered him a position at American Coffee right away, one notch higher than his position at American Pizza.

It was a tough decision, though exactly the kind of problem Joe wanted to have after he had gotten fired five years earlier, I suppose. When Joe asked me if he should take it, I said, "Definitely." I admitted that I hoped he would succeed me as the VP in charge of American Pizza, if and when I got promoted to American Foods, but I said there really was no telling if that was ever going to happen. I didn't want him to wait around forever, cooling his heels. Besides, I added, if he did well at American Coffee, his chances would only be that much greater to head up American Pizza—or something else—in the future.

"And who knows," I said, "you might like it better. Starting something yourself can be exciting—trust me."

Needless to say, Joe took the job—and he tells me I was right: starting something yourself is a blast! American Coffee faced a lot of obstacles embarking on such a new path, trying to convince the American public that this is the way to drink coffee, but they've come through in a big way. Now American Coffee is at the top of the field—and the most profitable of all the American Foods divisions, including American Pizza!

Because of our demanding jobs running two of the company's top divisions, Joe and I gradually found it harder and harder to keep in touch with each other. But when I heard his voice on the radio, it snapped me out of the doldrums like that, and I knew I had to call my old friend the minute I got into the office. Heck, if I was really going to go through with it and quit my job, I might as well tell one of my oldest friends about it first.

I asked to meet him for lunch and naturally suggested American Pizza, but Joe coaxed me to come over to the American Coffee shop on the first floor of his office building for a morning perk-up. With 30 minutes before our meeting, I also had time to draw up my resignation, a simple little thing in which I wrote: "To whom it may concern: I, Larry Hogan, hereby submit my resignation from my current post as vice president of American Foods, in charge of the American Pizza division, simply because I no longer feel I am as effective as I should be in this role, and therefore no longer derive the enjoyment from my work that I once did. Sincerely, Larry Hogan."

I wrote it out so easily, without even a revision. I looked at it, exhaled in relief, and slipped it into the top drawer of my desk. I knew enough not to submit it immediately without pausing to think about it, but I still felt a tremendous load lift off of me. I was amazed at how I could do something I never thought I'd do in a million years, and do it without much hesitation. But to be sure it was the right decision, I knew I'd have to think it through—or even better, talk it through with an old friend.

*To whom it may concern:
I, Larry Hogan, hereby submit my
resignation from my current post
as vice president of American
Foods, in charge of the American
Pizza division, simply because I no
longer feel I am as effective as I
should be in this role, and therefore
no longer derive the enjoyment
from my work that I once did.*

Sincerely, Larry Hogan

COFFEE BREAK

I showed up at Joe's office at nine o'clock, as we'd agreed, so we could catch up a bit before heading down to the shop. Joe was dressed professionally, as always. He had a well-deserved reputation as a sharp dresser—not flashy, but a classic look with style and panache. He seemed light, happy, relaxed, and energetic—just as I had been five years earlier. But when I caught a glimpse of myself in a mirror in Joe's office, my face told another story. My graying hair matched my graying complexion. I looked tired compared to Joe. The sparkle had left my eyes, and I felt my responses were all just a little sluggish compared to Joe's.

I suspect Joe asked me to meet him at his office so he could show me his corner spread and feel the happy hum of the workplace. His goal certainly wasn't to gloat—that's not Joe's style—and my office was still bigger and more opulent in any case. I think he just wanted to show me what my former protégé had accomplished.

"You're doing well, my friend," I said, gazing over the office.

"I owe it all to you, Sensei," Joe replied. "Without your guidance on Six Sigma on the worst day of my life, I wouldn't have any of this, and this division wouldn't look anything like what you see here today. I just wanted you to see it."

We talked a bit about our families, our favorite football teams, and a few mutual friends, then headed down for some coffee.

Joe opened the door, which provided some quick aromatherapy for a confirmed coffee fiend. "Where shall we sit?" I asked, thinking he might have a favorite table.

"Anywhere you like," Joe answered. "Our customers have told us that's how they like it."

"Don't some of your waitstaff get overwhelmed if we all sit in the same section?"

"Not at all," Joe said. "We decided to ditch the traditional 'my section' method right off the bat for what we call the Rover System, which works just like the outfield in Little League baseball. Everyone gets to every table they can. You'll never hear one of these waiters say, 'Sorry, you're not in my section. I'll get your waitress,' because *everyone* is your waitress here!"

"Makes sense to me," I said. "I guess you're right, now that I think about it. The customers never really care what your job description is. All they want is service, as soon as they can get it."

"Bingo," Joe said. "And as you know, that's what we're trying to do here: whatever the *customer* wants."

As if on cue, our waitress came up to take our order. "Hello Joe," she said. "Who's your friend?"

"Hello Sandra," Joe said. "This is Larry, an old buddy of mine from our days at American Burger." I could tell he was about to mention that I was also the executive vice president in charge of American Pizza, but I gave him a subtle hand signal to stop him from divulging my title. Discretion was another quality of Joe's I admired.

"Hello, Larry. I'm Sandra."

"Hello, Sandra. Nice to meet you."

"Do you guys know what you want?"

"Well, I bet you know what *I* want," Joe said.

"Café Latte coming up, Mr. Meter! And you sir?"

"Hmmm. What's your favorite, Sandra?"

"Oh, the Café Mocha is delicious. But you can't go wrong with Joe's favorite, the Café Latte, either."

"Nice job kissing up, Sandra," Joe joked. We all laughed.

"Well, I try," she said with a grin. "So, what'll it be?"

"Café Latte and a scone for me, please," Joe said.

"And a Café Mocha for me," I said. "You sold me."

"Anything else?"

Joe looked at me, and I shook my head. "Think that'll do it for now," Joe said.

"Alright, let me go get those for you," Sandra said, and she was off.

"Great service," I said. "Of course, it pays to be the king."

Joe chuckled. "Well, maybe. But honestly, you'd get the same service no matter who you were. We've put a lot of systems into place to make sure we hire, train, and retain the best waitstaff around, and we reward them for great service and teamwork. That doesn't mean what you just experienced happens automatically, but I'm pleased to say, it seems to happen a lot more often here than at other coffee shops."

"I'd guess so. How'd you set all this up?"

"Oh, we can get to that later," Joe said. Right then, Sandra returned with our orders. "Café Latte for Mr. Meter, and a Café Mocha for Mr. Larry," she said, setting them down on inviting cardboard coasters before us. "And a cinnamon stick for you, Mr. Meter, and a chocolate cookie stick for you, Mr. Larry."

"A little VIP treatment?" I asked, thinking I'd caught Sandra treating us differently because the division head was there.

"Don't flatter yourself," Sandra joked. "I hate to tell you, but we do this for all our customers."

"And why is that, Sandra?" Joe asked, giving Sandra the setup she needed to recite one of American Coffee's advertising slogans.

"Because they told us they like it," Sandra said. "And that's enough for us."

"Ah, yes," I said. "Good campaign."

"Actually, the line was first delivered by Julie, one of our waitresses here," Sandra explained. "And we all liked it. It made sense to us. So we all started saying it, too. And it became our reason for doing almost everything we do."

"And, it also became our reason for *not* doing just about anything we thought the customers *wouldn't* like," Joe added. "For us, it's just that straightforward. If the customers will like something, we do it. If they won't like it, we don't do it. And even if they don't care about it either way, we don't do it. If any initiative we take won't eventually create some noticeable benefit that the customer will care about, we drop it. And whatever they like, we simply do more of. And that's how what used to be a treat," Joe concluded, picking up his cinnamon stick, "became standard procedure at every American Coffee shop."

"Hmmm," I said. "More than a slogan for you guys, I guess."

"I hope so!" Joe said. "Thanks, Sandra," Joe added, as she whisked off to another table.

Velocity versus Acceleration

"How's your Café Mocha?" Joe asked.

"It's great!" I said, savoring each sip, the aroma rising from the tall cup. "I admit it, I don't drink your coffee as much as I would like. I tell myself I'm too busy, so I usually just pick up a cup of whatever they're selling at the nearest donut drive-up window."

"Tsk, tsk," Joe joked. "See what you're missing?"

"Boy, do I!" I exclaimed. "This is fantastic! The coffee flavor is rich, but so is the chocolate—and neither overpowers the other. How do you do it?"

"Great beans and great chocolate!" Joe cracked. "Also, great water. People always underestimate that. But we can talk more about all that in a bit. I'd forgotten how fun it is to talk business with you."

"Well, business hasn't been as much fun lately," I said, which gave me the opening I needed to discuss the malaise I felt mired in.

"Why not?"

"Oh, lots of things, I guess," I said. "Don't get me wrong. American Pizza isn't going under, and I'm in no danger of losing my job . . . I think!"

"Unlike a former American Burger manager a few years ago, eh?" Joe said, joking about his own dismissal.

"Man, that seems like a long time ago, doesn't it?"

"Yes, it does—thank God!" Joe said, "but it was only a few years ago. Time does fly when you're having fun."

"Maybe that's my problem," I said. "It just hasn't been as much fun lately, not like it was. It's gotten so bad, Joe, I've got to admit, I'm actually thinking of quitting. Today."

"Whoa, really?" Joe said. "Seems like it's coming out of nowhere—to me, at least. Where'd this come from?"

"Well, there are a lot of reasons, I suppose," I said. "But the main one is simple: I don't think I'm doing a good job. We're not going anywhere, and it's just not fun anymore. And I'm not sure why."

"Do you have any hunches?" Joe asked.

"Maybe that's why I wanted to talk with you, to help sort it out."

"Let's start at the top," Joe said. "What's changed about your job since we had lunch five years ago, when you were so fired up about American Pizza and Six Sigma?"

"Not much, really, I guess," I said. "I mean, we're still doing well, and I'm still doing well. But it's just not the same. It doesn't feel fresh anymore. We're doing the same things over and over, and we aren't really getting any better—not any worse, mind you, but not any better either."

"I see," Joe said. "Stagnation. Steady as she goes."

"Yeah, pretty much," I said. "Our profits are still good but haven't improved in five quarters. Our employee turnover isn't bad, but it's not getting any better either. Same could be said for our stock price, our customer satisfaction ratings, our reputation, you name it. All good, just not getting *better,* the way I want it to be."

"Sigmund Freud said that no matter how happy you are, you adjust to your level of happiness, and then you want to be happier," Joe said. "If you just got a raise to $50,000, that's great and you're thrilled. But you get used to it after a while, your expenses grow, and then you want more. So you're thrilled when you hit $100,000, but you get used to that, too, and adjust accordingly—and so on and so on.

It's not just velocity that excites us, it's *acceleration!* And no matter how fast you're going, if you're not accelerating, it feels like you're standing still."

"I guess that's it," I said. I already felt a little relieved just to get some of this off my chest with someone I could trust, and who would understand. "It feels like we're standing still, and after a while that can get to you."

"Feel like you're growing barnacles?" Joe asked, with a smile.

I laughed again, which I had done more of this morning than I had in weeks, if not months. "'Fraid so! How do you scrape them off the hull and get the ship moving again? You guys seem to be going up, up, up!"

"Before I answer that one, can I ask you one?"

"Sure," I said. "Fire away."

"How's your Sigma rating?"

"We're at about a Five Sigma," I said.

"So you're still making about 250 mistakes for every million opportunities?" Joe asked. "Yep," I said. "Of course, that's not bad. Better than our competition, and it took us a while to get there."

"Not bad at all," Joe agreed. "But what's driving you nuts is that you're stuck there, aren't you?"

I chuckled. "Yeah, pretty much. I guess since I first talked with you over our infamous lunch, American Pizza has plateaued. And, how'd you know we stalled at Five Sigma? Have you got moles?"

The Wall

"No moles, it's just easy to predict," Joe said. "Happens to the best of us, my friend. You have no more loyal convert to Six Sigma than me, Larry. You did a great job explaining it to me, showing how it all worked, even inspiring me. When I started here at American Coffee, Six Sigma helped us eliminate a flurry of recurring mistakes, from the way we produced our coffee to the way we delivered it to the customers to the way we kept track of the money coming in. In the process, we improved morale, customer satisfaction, and profits—all good goals. And important ones, too. We both know that our two divisions wouldn't be half of what they are today without Six Sigma. But I've discovered something: Using the concepts of Six Sigma alone, you really can't get beyond Five Sigma. No one really does."

"A bit ironic," I said, "given the name."

Joe smiled. "True enough. You know and I know the incredible triumphs corporations have achieved through Six Sigma, but there seems to be a barrier at Five Sigma that even the best companies can't get past—sort of like the 'runner's wall' marathoners smack into about 20 miles into the race. But what's really getting to you, I'll bet, is how banging your head against the Five Sigma wall drains you."

> **U**sing the concepts of Six Sigma alone, you really can't get beyond Five Sigma. No one really does.

I raised my eyebrows and nodded. "I guess that's really it. We keep getting the same results again and again, and no matter how good they are, I'm not inspired. I feel ineffective, even useless. What's the point of being the captain of a ship that's just bobbing around at sea, going nowhere? I feel like I could take my hand off the rudder now, and we wouldn't miss a thing."

"But as you said before, you're maintaining at Five Sigma," Joe countered, trying to buck me up. "You're still running one of the best brand names in the business."

"I guess you're right," I said, "and I probably need the reminder. But that's not how it feels."

"That I understand," Joe said, "because I was feeling the exact same thing two years ago, when we hit Five Sigma at American Coffee and then discovered we just couldn't budge past it, no matter what we did."

"Why do you think that is?" I asked.

"Good question," Joe said. "A few reasons, I suppose. For one thing, in business you can only get so far by picking the 'low-hanging fruit.' By that I mean designing Six Sigma projects to correct the biggest cost-guzzling problems you have that yield the greatest savings and customer satisfaction. Sooner or later, you have to go for the tougher stuff."

"So what'd you do?" I asked.

"We went back to school," Joe said. "Back to the school of Six Sigma. I wasn't looking for the great Unifying Theory of Business—but I feel like I found it, anyway, by accident. Want me to tell you what I learned?"

I laughed. "You kidding? Throw me a life jacket here, man! I'm drowning!"

"Well, Lord knows, I owe you one and then some," Joe said. "And who knows? Maybe by the end of our little coffee break here, you'll be as jacked up as I was after having lunch with you five years ago."

"Boy, I hope!"

"Okay," I said, "here goes."

Not Just for Engineers Anymore

"Despite its name," Joe said, "implementing Six Sigma can only take a company so far, which is what you told me at the end of our infamous lunch five years ago. Organizations that want to reach the next level of efficiency need to adopt a program called Design for Six Sigma, or DFSS, as you call it."

"Boy, that's right," I said, as it all came back to me. "I was just starting to look into DFSS at that point, but I got sidetracked. I can't remember why, now."

"Well, let me guess," Joe said. "You were so caught up in the day-to-day problems, you never had time to look up to see where you were going."

I had to laugh at that image. "I'm sure that was it. Six Sigma itself was keeping us plenty busy. It's like biking up a mountain road. You're peddling so hard, you just look down at your feet and not at the horizon."

*I*mplementing Six Sigma can only take a company so far. Organizations that want to reach the next level of efficiency need to adopt a program called Design for Six Sigma, or DFSS.

"Good analogy," Joe said. "I'm stealing it!"

"All yours," I offered. "Now, refresh my memory. Design for Six Sigma—is that Six Sigma for engineers?"

"Well, it works for engineers," Joe said. "*Design* often gives the wrong idea, because a lot of people assume right off the bat that it's for engineers, and only engineers. Not so! A better word may be *development,* but unfortunately I didn't name it, I just use it!

"For starters," Joe continued, "when you think about it with an open mind, design itself is not the private domain of engineers. Design is everyone's business. Our jobs may or may not be designed for us, but we design how we perform them."

"Amen," I said.

> **D**esign itself is not the private domain of engineers. Design is everyone's business. Our jobs may or may not be designed for us, but we design how we perform them.

Joe laughed. "Sometimes I forget that I'm not talking to the same stubborn nonbeliever of a few years ago—me! Boy, I must've been a tough sell."

"You weren't ready to listen, at first," I admitted kindly. "But, obviously, you came around. And as they say, there's no more fervent believer than a convert."

"So true," Joe said. "Well, back to my point about design. It doesn't matter who you are or what your official title is. If you're working, you're designing. We design projects. We design processes. We design presentations, reports, and plans. I firmly believe that Design for Six Sigma can be effectively and successfully applied to virtually every activity we perform every day."

> **I**f you're working, you're designing. I firmly believe that Design for Six Sigma can be effectively and successfully applied to virtually every activity we perform every day.

"For example?"

"Oh, jeez, there are hundreds!" Joe said. "You can use DFSS to design a more cost-effective, error-free overnight delivery system. Or a lighter-weight, more-durable hubcap that doesn't bend or break when you hit a pothole. Or, say, a more streamlined internal mail system for your company that reduces misdirected interoffice mail. Or a cleaner, more-pleasing presentation software that's easier to use. For us, it meant designing a better floor plan, a better menu, and a better benefits package for our employees. These design changes allowed us to implement our Rover System, one of the keys to our success. The point is: Designing isn't just for engineers anymore."

THE CRUCIAL DIFFERENCES

"I get the picture," I said. "So why do we need DFSS, when we've already got Six Sigma?"

"You might as well ask why football teams need to pass the ball when they already know how to run it. Even extreme efforts can only push performance levels as high as 5.5 Sigma, but when you try such Herculean efforts, you invariably get diminishing returns, because the costs eventually threaten to wipe out any savings you might get from pushing it that far. And that's why companies like GE, AlliedSignal, Caterpillar, and all the rest are investing at least as much time, personnel, and money into Design for Six Sigma as they did for Six Sigma."

"We've already implemented Six Sigma at American Pizza, of course," I said, "but I'm curious, if we hadn't, would we have to do Six Sigma before doing DFSS?"

"Good question," Joe said. "It breaks down like this: Many business leaders view DFSS as the obvious sequel to Six Sigma, the second leg of this business biathlon they need to complete for their companies to reach their full potential. DFSS is already shaping up to be just as popular as Six Sigma. Anywhere that Six Sigma goes, DFSS is sure to follow, but in some cases, DFSS should actually come *first,* before Six Sigma—despite what Six Sigma promoters would have you believe. Six Sigma is *not* a prerequisite for Design for Six Sigma. In fact, DFSS is not even dependent on Six Sigma."

"So what's the difference between Six Sigma and DFSS?"

"Well, let's take Six Sigma first," Joe said. "You know as well as I do the idea behind Six Sigma is simple: Instead of simply plugging leak after leak, the idea is to figure out *why* it's leaking and *where*—and attack the problem at its source. But Six Sigma doesn't address the original *design* of the product or process; it merely improves on them."

"Go on," I said.

"Okay," he said. "DFSS is not simply a rehash of the lessons learned in Six Sigma but a fundamentally different approach to business. Design for Six Sigma complements the Six Sigma improvement methodology, but DFSS takes it one step farther—or really, one step *back,* ferreting out the flaws of the product and the process during the upstream design stage, *not* the quality control stage or even the production stage. While Six Sigma focuses on improving *existing* designs, DFSS concentrates its efforts on *creating new and better ones.*"

"Alright, I'm interested," I said, "but you'll need to elaborate."

"In layman's terms—the only kind I know!—the difference between Six Sigma and DFSS is the difference between getting a tune-up and a brand-new engine or between patching your pants and getting a new pair. It's the difference between having to add cream to your coffee, because it's too bitter, and making better coffee from better beans in the first place. Instead of constantly 'debugging' products and processes that already exist—an effort that never ends, of course—DFSS starts from scratch to design the product or process to be virtually error-free in the first place. This effectively replaces the usual trial-and-error approach with a cleaner end result that also requires much less after-market tinkering."

The difference between Six Sigma and DFSS is the difference between getting a tune-up and a brand-new engine or between patching your pants and getting a new pair.

"Ah," I said, with index finger raised. "The classic 'pay me now or pay me later' option. You spend more time and effort up front so you have to spend less down the road."

"Exxxactly!" Joe said. "When I worked as a carpenter—before I met you in the American Foods mail room—my boss always said, 'Measure twice and cut once.' Sure beats the other way around! And that's what Design for Six Sigma is all about: getting it right the first time. If the design or process is flawed in the first place, you can only do so much with downstream fixes. And that's why no one can really get past Five Sigma with Six Sigma alone.

"Hmmm. I'm beginning to understand why we're stuck."

"Oh, but that's not all!" Joe said, imitating a Ginsu salesman. "Here's something that'll make you think, a new way of looking at things I learned from DFSS: Manufacturing can only *take quality away* from the design, not improve it, so we must do our best to make the design as flawless as possible before we start cranking out the widgets."

"Forget the widgets," I said. "Show me something from the real world."

"Alright," Joe said, taking the challenge. "Let's say you start out with an ideal notion of a car. It's always perfect on the computer, of course, no squeaks or rattles. But you start banging steel and snapping on bumpers and getting human hands all over it, and the *best* you can hope for is to *match* the ideal computer design—never exceed it. But as we know, very few cars even come close. The key is to *design* the car and the processes that create it so the flaws can never occur in the first place. And that's what DFSS is set up to do."

"Works for me," I said. "Spend more time and effort on preparing the recipe, and less time and effort trying to mask the mistakes after it comes out of the oven. But again, DFSS sounds like it's made for manufacturing."

"Not true, my friend," Joe said. "All of that applies to processes, too, from streamlining the gas station experience to the way we get our customers through the line or served at their tables right here at American Coffee. With DFSS, you design the processes so they are debugged from the outset and stay that way, and then you're not always putting out fires after the fact."

"I'm with you," I said. "So, if I have it right, Six Sigma helps fix what's broken, but Design for Six Sigma helps design things that don't break in the first place, things that do more and cost less. Upstream problem prevention as opposed to downstream problem solving."

"That's it!" Joe said, pleased at how quickly I got the point. "In a nutshell, things can get fixed in the short term with Six Sigma, and replaced in the long term with Design for Six Sigma. If your company were a house, it'd work like this: While most business initiatives would focus only on plugging leaky pipes and fixtures, a Six Sigma approach would examine the process and discover that the quality of the welding and sink faucets was inadequate and replace them. DFSS would take one step back in the process by designing the system—before it was ever installed—with welds and fixtures it knew would produce Six Sigma quality, without repairs or redesigns down the road.

"Of course, few businesses involve leaky pipes," Joe continued. "But all businesses involve customers, and understanding how to please and even thrill them is the key, naturally, to the success of any business you can name. Too many companies don't take the time or make the effort to learn what their customers really want. Through methods we learned from DFSS, we know how to find out what customers really want and then use this information to meet the needs and desires of these customers. This works whether the customer is external—a consumer who buys our coffee, for example—or internal, like Sandra."

"Okay, I think I get it," I said. "DFSS is a means to purify the product—or process!—before you put it into place, because you design it with the end in mind, which is customer satisfaction."

"Yeah, exactly," Joe said. "I do believe you've got it!"

"But I gotta say, it sounds like a lot of work, maybe even more than the Six Sigma projects," I said. "Wouldn't it require too much work and money to start DFSS projects on every aspect of a company's business?"

"Not to worry," Joe said, anticipating my objection. "The good news is, not everything that companies do *needs* to achieve Six Sigma performance levels. But for products such as airplanes and automobile tires, where achieving Six Sigma quality can literally be a matter of life and death, Design for Six Sigma comes to the rescue. It's also vital for companies fighting for customers in highly competitive fields, including virtually all companies in the high-tech or service industries, where you have to battle a ton of good businesses for the right to satisfy increasingly demanding customers. All these tasks are tough and, therefore, ripe for DFSS projects.

"At American Coffee, we don't focus on hitting Six Sigma in everything we do," Joe continued. "We have to pick our battles. You might have noticed that we look overstaffed, for example. I'll talk more about this in a bit, if you like. We decided to emphasize service over payroll, because we figured if we're going to charge customers almost four bucks for a cup of coffee, we better get it to them fast! And besides, we realized it just makes good business sense for us never to make them wait to give us four bucks."

"Good thinking!" I said.

"Actually," Joe admitted, "I got the idea from Vegas. You notice that no one ever waits to play blackjack. There always seems to be an extra table or two open. And it makes sense: why should customers wait in line to give them money? So, we're Six Sigma on coffee quality and service but not on keeping our staff expenditures down to the bone. Of course, they do other things if they don't have customers, but I'll save that for later, too.

"What floors me," Joe added, "is the fact that most companies spend only 5 percent of their budget on design, when design typically would determine 70 percent of the cost of the product—partly because 80 percent of all quality problems are unwittingly *designed into* the product itself. In fact, in government contracts, 30 to 40 percent of the budget is set aside for testing and correcting the product—after-market measures. Imagine! So they're admitting in advance that one-third of the budget must be devoted to correcting the problems they plan to create with the first two-thirds of the budget! My gut says, any time testing and fixing are planned for up front, it is a virtual certainty that testing and fixing will be performed. Plan for failure, and you'll get it."

> *Eighty percent of all quality problems are unwittingly **designed into** the product itself.*

"Hear! Hear!" I said.

"DFSS rejects all this old-school thinking," Joe asserted, clearly on a roll. "The DFSS approach leads to 'clean' designs that dramatically reduce the need for later inspection, testing, and reworking. It corrects the biggest reason, I believe, that the old way is so slow and expensive. When I was a carpenter, I learned about something called 'accrued error,' which occurs when you make a slightly faulty measurement while you're building the foundation, and that mistake gets magnified every time you build the next thing on top of it. By the time you're working on the roof, everything is so off-kilter you're forced to scrap your original plans and find a way to make the roof joists fit any way you can. 'Jury-rigging' it like that might help you get the job done, at least in the short term, but you're going to get a ton of problems down the road when your roof leaks and everything else starts falling apart."

"As the owner of an older home, I know exactly what you're talking about!" I said. "I often think it would be cheaper simply to bulldoze my 80-year-old house and start from scratch."

We both chuckled. "The scary part is, you might be right!" Joe said. "In companies that don't follow DFSS, the 'firefighters' who correct these endless errors as they crop up are the heroes of the organization, when the real heroes should be the people who focus on prevention in the first place. Although fire prevention is not as dramatic as fire fighting, it's a lot cheaper, easier, and more efficient."

"You said it," I said. "Sometimes I think of that when I think of the 9-11 tragedy—how we might have prevented it."

"I think we all probably do," Joe said. "Like everyone else, I'm still stunned by the incredible heroism and selflessness of the New York firefighters, running up those stairs to help those who were stranded when they knew they were tempting disaster. But I also think of the countless ways we could have prevented those firefighters ever having to do that in the first place. The people who ensure our nation's security and who are doing their jobs well don't get headlines—but they still carry the burden of preventing disastrous headlines from ever occurring!"

"I see your point," I said. "And I couldn't agree more. But how does this relate to DFSS? What's the upshot?" I asked, always eager to get to the bottom line.

"The upshot is this: DFSS companies spend a lot more time and money during the design phase than the traditional 5 percent that most companies spend.

By spending more up front, however, they can dramatically shrink the 70 percent other companies spend for the finished products or services they create. The goal is to replace as many inspectors as possible and put producers in their place. After all, it's the producers who produce the product and make the money, which creates a very cost-effective trade-off. You get fewer changes in your original plans downstream, and avoid the countless ad hoc decisions so many companies are forced to make. You also spend less on resources, since there's less waste, and you get the intangible benefit of having all your employees committed to the entire project, not just their piece of the pie," Joe said.

"Boy, that all sounds pretty good to me!" I said. "I think American Pizza could use a nice injection of this approach—and maybe I could, too!"

"Well, the best part for you, my friend, is that DFSS has already been tried and proven to work as advertised. Motorola applied DFSS to the design and production of one of their recent pagers, and according to *Consumer Reports,* it's virtually defect-proof. General Electric enrolled 20,000 of their employees in the DFSS program, so they could perfect everything from engine blades to responding to phone calls about service. And it has worked like a charm."

> **G**eneral Electric enrolled 20,000 of their employees in the DFSS program, so they could perfect everything from engine blades to responding to phone calls about service.

"Alright, you've got me," I said. "So how does it work exactly? Give me the nuts and bolts of it. And most important, where do I start?"

PUTTING OUR BEST FOOT FORWARD

"Mao Tse-tung said the longest march begins with a single step," Joe said. "No matter how daunting the journey, the important thing is to get started."

"Hear! Hear!" I said. The idea of starting—of starting anything, sometimes—can pull us out of the ruts we find ourselves in occasionally. Certainly, the idea of starting something new sounded good to me.

"But there's a catch," Joe said. "When you're launching DFSS, it's absolutely vital to make sure the first step is a good one, because if it's not, you might not get another chance. As you know, Larry, American employees are understandably weary of the endless management theories. That's why it's crucial that a company's first DFSS project succeeds."

"How can you possibly guarantee success," I asked, "especially on your first DFSS project, when everyone's still figuring out how it works?"

"Hey," Joe said. "You know and I know you can never guarantee success—at anything. There are no sure things in this world. But there are a lot of things you can do to increase your odds of succeeding on that first project."

"Such as?"

Joe laughed. "I was ready for that. First, you need to pick a juicy target for your initial DFSS project. The fatter your target, the better your chances."

"So what's a good target?" I asked. "Just setting up some fish in a barrel for shooting practice?"

"Well, it can't just be a slam dunk," Joe said. "It's got to be innovative enough to capture your employees' imaginations, but straightforward enough to make sure a solid effort will succeed. No layups, but no half-court shots, either."

"Okay," I said, enjoying the role of interrogator for a change. "What did you guys start out with here?"

"For our first DFSS project at American Coffee, we wanted to solve our biggest problem first, and that was speed. If you go into almost any fancy coffee shop, you stand in line for five or ten minutes, even when there are only a few customers."

"Been there, done that," I said. "That's one of my frustrations about most of the new coffee shops. It takes forever!"

"Bingo!" Joe said. "We discovered that in the average coffee shop—including ours!—the average line was four people deep, and the average wait was ten minutes! Two and a half minutes for each customer—just for a cup of coffee, for cryin' out loud!"

"Amen!" I said. I never could understand why the same people who could brew such sophisticated coffee could also be so backwards when it came to getting it in their customers' hands faster.

"So that was our first project: cutting down the customer waiting time," Joe said. "A juicy target, and an important one. We *had* to improve the experience of everyone involved—customers, employees, and managers—and also improve our bottom line."

"Alright," I said. "I think I've got it: you pick a juicy target, but one worth going for. Not too hard and not too easy, but with a big payoff."

"That's it," Joe said. "I do believe you've got it."

"Now," I said, rubbing my hands together, "how do you tackle that one?"

"In due time, my friend," I said. "There's more to learn first."

"Such as?"

"How to launch it. Before we even get to the steps, we've got to make sure the first step is a solid one."

"Lead me, Sensei!" I joked, and Joe laughed before jumping into the topic.

"I don't want to spend too much time on this, because you can get more detailed information from books," he said. "In a nutshell, to get started right you need five things: a strong commitment from the top executives; training for the masses; effective communications vertically and horizontally about what you're up to; a sound integration strategy, to make sure what you're doing becomes a part of the organization; and a focus, as always, on bottom-line performance, which drives the whole process."

"So far, so good," I said.

"Good," Joe said. "I don't need to lecture you about getting the top brass onboard. We both know from our own experience, and Six Sigma, that we can't expect our people to do anything we're not willing to do. There aren't many successful coaches who never played the games they coach. They may or may not have been great athletes themselves."

"Thank you very much," I joked, raising my hand.

"But they know what it takes to make a pressure shot, to make a tackle, or to try to hit a curveball. And that's how they teach their players. Employees will rarely dedicate themselves to a new project unless they see the CEO believing in it, too. There is no substitute for enthusiasm. A good coach has to earn the respect and commitment of his players. That's how good executives do it, too."

> *Employees will rarely dedicate themselves to a new project unless they see the CEO believing in it, too.*

"You're right, it's a simple point," I said, "but one you've got to stress. When we were kids, we all knew from our parents' behavior what they really believed in and what they didn't—no matter what they told us. The same goes for our employees."

"Exactly," Joe said. "It's not enough for us to give it lip service. We have to put our most valuable commodity, our TIME, where our mouths are. And the most important place for an executive to spend his time is on the DFSS rollout, the very start of the process. It takes about three months, and if we do it right, our people will understand DFSS, especially what it takes to overcome the obstacles we almost always face in starting a great initiative and a rollout plan that works.

"In our case," Joe added, "that was pretty easy, because obviously the top brass (he points a thumb at himself) was the *main* guy onboard. No one had to convince me. But that's something to keep an eye on. If you don't have that buy-in from the top, you're finished from the start."

"Nice play on words," I said.

"It's a specialty," Joe replied, raising his coffee cup in a mock toast. "Another key point: The rollout should focus on projects, just like Six Sigma did, instead of vague improvements. As I said before, there are a lot of differences between Six Sigma and DFSS, but the initial techniques are very similar. How we APPLY those techniques will separate the two, but for now, you know what I'm talking about."

"Well, I can appreciate why you're taking the launch so seriously," I said. "As they say, you don't get a second chance to make a first impression."

"That's it," Joe said. "That's it exactly."

"Hey guys," Sandra said, returning to our table. "Can I get you anything else?" She breezily picked up the loose items on our table as she spoke, leaving our half-filled cups in place.

"I would like some water, actually, if it's not too much trouble," I said.

" It's my job," Sandra said with a smile. "So no, not TOO much trouble! Now, what kind of water would you like, sparkling or regular?"

"Oh, regular's fine," I said. "No need to spend good money on bottled water."

"Well, they're both bottled," she said. "And they're both free, so don't worry about the money."

"Ah, it's good to hang out with the king," I said.

"Oh, it's not free as a special favor to Joe. Once again, you overestimate my boss," she joked. "It's free for anyone who buys a cup of coffee."

"You're kidding," I said. "That stuff costs two or three bucks at every other place in town. It's got to be a huge moneymaker."

"I'm sure it is," Joe said. "But doesn't it tick you off to pay that kind of money for WATER?"

"Of course it does!" I said. "And man, you can't tell the difference from one brand to the next."

"That's what we found," Joe said. "We actually did a taste test in the store, and no one could distinguish any of them. We also polled our customers, ALL of whom said the price of water was ludicrous. So, we thought about it and decided that we're already charging top dollar for the coffee here—which the customers accept, because they can tell it's much better than other coffee—so why do we need to gouge them on water? It's a little thing, but it makes our customers feel respected."

"I agree," I said. "I think it's a great move for PR. Your customers must love it. But what about the bottom line? Surely you have to pay the supplier, who's still going to make an unbelievable profit from it."

Sandra smiled. "So you'd think. Well, Mr. Joe and his minions started looking into it, and they learned that there's almost nothing to the bottled water business. If you can find a good spring—and there are thousands in the U.S.—and you can filter it, bottle it, and ship it—things we already do with other products anyway—you can enter the bottled water business without spending much money at all."

"Sandra's right," Joe said. "The real cost of entry into that field is advertising. It's huge. But we didn't want to sell our water in grocery stores for a nice profit. We wanted to GIVE IT AWAY—and you don't need to advertise to do that!"

I laughed. "No, I suppose not! So, it's a nice goodwill gesture that doesn't cost too much, which is good business."

"Even better," Sandra continued, grinning. "We need good water anyway to make our coffee. It's the most underestimated ingredient to a good cup, because good beans can never completely overcome bad water. And we deliver a lot more coffee than water. We use over 90 percent of our spring water for our coffee and put only 10 percent in bottles."

"We used to have to pay our supplier for that water," Joe said, "but by pumping it ourselves, we cut out the middleman, saving a ton of money. So we've saved a lot by doing it this way—so much that we can easily afford to give you bottled water for free."

"I'll be," I said, under my breath. "And you get a great ad campaign out of it to boot. 'At American Coffee, we start brewing your cup 500 feet below ground.' You remember that!"

"And I bet you remember, 'Where is the water in YOUR coffee coming from?'" Joe said, referring to another campaign where the dubious practices of other coffee companies were mocked.

"Of course," I said. "A classic. But hey, haven't I seen your water in grocery stores, too?"

Sandra laughed. "Darn, you got us! Well, an employee here had the bright idea to sell the stuff in stores anyway, since our brand name was already so strong and we had built up goodwill from giving it away in our stores. We figured, Why not? We're already bottling water anyway, and we can easily sell it for 25 percent less than our less scrupulous competitors."

"And this is the beauty part," Joe said. "In addition to all the other PR and economic and quality benefits I've told you about, thanks to our relatively modest but solid sales of bottled water in the grocery stores, we're actually making money in the water business itself anyway. Everything else is gravy!"

We all laughed at that. "In that case," I said, "I would surely like a bottled water, please."

"Comin' right up, Mr. Larry!"

"There's a point to that story, though," Joe said. "Every step in that process was driven by DFSS. And now I'll show you how."

First Things First

"Part of the program, you already know, and know well," Joe said. "Like all teams, your DFSS team needs different players doing different jobs. Any good football coach will tell you the same thing: Every player must have a specific role, clearly defined, with consequences for not coming through and rewards for doing his particular job well. And that goes for everyone in the organization, from the quarterback to the water boy."

"Just like Six Sigma," I said, something I knew well.

"Of course," Joe said. "In fact, you'll be relieved to know that the roles are virtually the same. Care to name them for me?"

"Sure," I said, always up for a challenge. "You've got the Executive Leadership at the top, who've got to buy into the program or else no one else will—just what you said about taking the first step. You've got the Champions, the guys who clear out all the obstacles in the way. The Master Black Belts, of course, are the engines that make the whole thing move—the workhorses. Next come the Black Belts, the Master Black Belt understudies, and the Green Belts and Team Members, who serve as support staff for the entire enterprise."

"Well done!" Joe said. "But hey, since you taught me, maybe I should have expected you to get them all right."

"Jeez, let's hope!" I said.

"Okay, the players are the same as in Six Sigma," Joe said. "But the game plan is definitely different. Care to run through the Six Sigma game plan, Sensei?"

"In my sleep, grasshopper," I said. "It's DMAIC."

"Which stands for . . . ?"

"Dumb Managers Always Ignore Customers," I said, and we both chuckled. "Or, more formally, Define the problem, Measure where you stand, Analyze where the problem starts, Improve the situation, and Control the new process to confirm that it's fixed—DMAIC!"

"You win the spelling bee," Joe said. "Now, are you ready for the new game plan?"

"I'm ready," I said. "Fire!"

PROCESS POWER
OF DFSS

"Here goes!" Joe said. "DMAIC was great for streamlining existing processes—taking out the bugs and translation problems between divisions—without too much cost or disruption. But in DFSS, we replace DMAIC with something called IDDOV, which stands for: *Identify* and *Define* the opportunity, *Develop* the concept, and *Optimize* the design and *Verify* it. Of course, in some programs it's called DMADV, which stands for *Define, Measure, Analyze, Develop,* and *Ver-*

ify, or DMEDI, which stands for *Define, Measure, Explore, Design,* and *Implement.* It really doesn't matter, though. It's all DFSS, and it all revolves around a five-step program, just the way Six Sigma does."

> **D**FSS uses something called IDDOV. In some programs, it's called DMADV or DMEDI...but it really doesn't matter. It's all DFSS, and it all revolves around a five-step program.

"Alright," I said. "What's the difference between the DMAIC and IDDOV, boiled down?"

"Boiled down, it's the difference between Six Sigma and DFSS itself," Joe said, "which, as you remember, is the difference between improving what you've got and designing it to be flawless in the first place."

"In DFSS, we break down these five steps into two stages, with Identify and Define the Opportunity in the first stage, and Develop, Optimize, and Verify as the second. Roughly, planning followed by execution.

The purpose of Stage One is to provide strong, clear directions for the efforts to come. Needless to say, a small mistake here will have ripple effects and grow into ugly results down the road, like kinking the branch of a sapling to watch it become a deformed arm of an otherwise mighty oak. It's important to get this one right from the outset."

"I'm with you," I said. "Now, how does it break down, step-by-step?"

"From the top!" Joe said. "The main point of the Identify and Define the Opportunity stage is to get the project started on the right foot, which we've talked about some already, with clearly defined goals. Think of a journey with no destination, and you see the problem. Goals should be as specific as possible in order to improve the chances of achieving them."

"Setting the table," I said.

"Exactly. There are steps within the steps, of course, but you can learn all that by reading a book on DFSS I have back at the office."

The Pieces of the I-D Puzzle

"Sounds good," I said. "So what can you tell me now?"

"Basically," Joe said, "the key is to be as specific as possible before you dive in. The more you know about what you're trying to do, the better your chances of doing it. It's like the difference between driving to the Rockies and driving to Denver."

"Okay," I said. "What am I trying to be specific about?"

"Your project's scope, its objectives, its goals—not just the big ones, but the milestones along the way, which are a lot more important in DFSS than in Six Sigma, because DFSS projects tend to focus more on long-term results. You need smaller goals along the way to keep you going."

"Break the marathon down to a series of sprints," I said.

"That's the idea. Now, when you're trying to determine your objectives and goals, you want to keep in mind Customer Satisfaction, Savings, and Profits, among other things."

"Okay, that's the theory," I said. "Put it in practice."

"Let's take our first project—cutting down customer lines," Joe said. "Even before we opened, that's something we knew we wanted to do. That was our biggest complaint when we were customers at other coffee places—and we learned that other customers felt the same way. So the first thing we did was go over our list. Will cutting down the wait in line increase customer satisfaction? Absolutely, that's the whole point of this project. Will it create savings? Sure, fewer lost customers and happier customers generally mean you're paying for fewer 'corrections.' And profits? Obviously, the more people we can serve in an hour, the more money we make.

"Then we moved onto the Project Scope," Joe continued. "This defines just how big the project will be and what it will cover—like outlining the playing field with chalk before the game begins. It doesn't tell us exactly what's going to happen once the project begins, but it does tell us where the 'game is going to be played'."

"But things have to change as you go along, don't they?" I asked. "How can you commit yourself to exactly what you will and won't be doing before the game even starts?"

"Good questions," Joe said. "There's built-in flexibility. Think of it as a game of 'hotter, colder' and you get the idea. You usually need to adjust the scope a few times to get it right, just like a telescope. Almost no one hits the bull's-eye on the first try, nor should they be expected to. But it's still helpful to make an estimate, and from there you can adjust up or down as needed, until you get hot, hot, hot.

"Take the line project," Joe added. "We talked about cutting down the line every hour we're open. Then we realized the line changes during the day— who's in it and for how long. A freelance writer strolling in at ten o'clock has a different set of expectations than a businessman at 8:30. So, we decided to focus only on the morning rush from 7 to 9, which kept things a lot more manageable.

"And we also knew we weren't going to eliminate morning lines on our first day, so we put Project Milestones into our plans. Remember, Six Sigma projects are intended to fix existing products and processes, but DFSS projects are intended to reinvent the entire wheel, so they're going to take longer. If you want to keep morale and momentum up, and the project focused over the long haul, you've got to create these shorter-term milestones—and they also help keep the project on track along the way.

> **S**ix Sigma projects are intended to fix existing products and processes, but DFSS projects are intended to reinvent the entire wheel, so they're going to take longer.

"Sprinters don't need to break down their races into smaller segments, like you said earlier, because their races are too short for that. But talk to any marathon runner, and he'll tell you that if you want to win a 26-mile race, you have to break it down into smaller segments, with different goals for each segment. Do the miniraces right, and the long one will take care of itself."

"Makes perfect sense to me," I said. "So what'd you do?"

"Well, we decided to first measure how big the line was at various times of the two-hour span for a week, and then try to reduce it by 20 percent every two weeks, until no one had to wait in line more than three minutes."

"Wow, how the heck did you do that?" I asked.

"Patience, my friend!" Joe joked. "We're getting there. The method is as important as the result."

"Alright, so sum it up so far," I said.

> **T**he method is as important as the result.

"Good idea. Basically, the first step is all about coming up with a detailed, ambitious but manageable Project Plan, one that includes the project's objectives and goals, the scope of what you're addressing, and a timeline for getting it all done. I can't stress enough the need to be *specific,* and *to write it down!* Ideas that aren't written down float away. Putting them in writing makes them real. Things that are

written down happen; things that are merely dis-
cussed do not."

"Boy, isn't that the truth," I said. "That's why I
always carry this," I said, raising my notebook, which
I'd been jotting in occasionally as we spoke. "I always
think I'll remember a lot more than I do."

"So simple, but so smart," Joe said. "If you don't
write it down, you have to explain it again each time
someone asks, or worse, be at the mercy of someone
else explaining it for you. But if you write it down,
your Project Plan can speak for you when you're not
there. And let's face it, our companies are too big to
tell everyone what to do one-on-one. Besides, things
that are written down are taken seriously. Discus-
sions are not. It's the difference between making a
speech and writing a book: the book lasts, the speech
doesn't."

"I'm sorry, what was that?" I joked, raising my
head from my notebook. "I was too busy writing it
all down."

Listening to the Customer

"Seems to me, though," I said, "that getting this specific this early in the process would be difficult. How do you know where to set the marks?"

"Well, again," Joe said, "you set your marks, then adjust as you know more. But the smartest business-people don't decide for themselves what the requirements of the project should be; they ask the customer and then work backwards."

"Start with the end in mind," I said, citing a popular business theory.

> *The smartest businesspeople don't decide for themselves what the requirements of the project should be; they ask the customer.*

"That way you get to the end!" Joe said. "And you know, when we talk about customers, we're talking about both internal and external customers—your employees as well as the people who buy your product or service. As a rule, American companies don't pay enough attention to their 'internal customers,' and almost no employees are so noble that they can still be nice to the guy who walks in the door after they've been mistreated by their coworkers or bosses."

"Sure," I said, reassured that all of this was not foreign to me. "A good rule of thumb: Treat your coworkers and employees as you'd have them treat your customers. What comes around, goes around."

"Exactly," Joe said. "Plan on it.

"By asking them, we learned some surprising things," Joe continued. "The biggest things our internal customers want is not more money or easier work, but clear direction, appreciation, and a say in how the store works. They want to be heard!"

"Well, seems like it's a win-win," I said, "because when you ask them, they'll tell you how to run the store better."

"Hallelujah!" Joe said. "What a simple idea! You've already seen how our employee input has improved our ad campaign and our service. Most of our best improvements come from them, and that may be because they invest more to make their own ideas work.

"But back to the external customer for a moment," Joe continued. "Don't tell them what they want, ask them! We were surprised to discover just how much customers are willing to pay for a cup of coffee—provided it's top quality and made especially for them. And I was also surprised to learn how unwilling they are to wait in line! So we adjusted. We raised the price a bit, to pay for the changes they asked for in service. Do this right, and they'll keep coming back.

"And that, we discovered by crunching the numbers, is more important than advertising, by far. I read about an insurance company that figured out by decreasing customer defections by just 5 percent, profits actually increased by 25 percent. Then there's a big manufacturing company that determined a mere 1 percent increase in its customer repurchase rate—from 50 percent to 51 percent—produced an extra $100 million a year in profits! Now, our numbers aren't like that, but percentagewise, it's the same."

"Well, like we've always said, defense is not as thrilling as offense, but it's just as important—maybe more so," I said. "At American Pizza, we still catch ourselves being too worried about getting the guy who's going to Pizza Hut, and not about keeping the guy already in our store."

"We all do," Joe said. "It's human nature to take for granted the gains we've already made. But customers have choices and can always change their minds."

"Alright, I have a question," I said. "How do we know what customers want?"

"Ask them, of course!" Joe said. "But you knew that. The first step is to distinguish between customer *needs* and customer *wants,* which are not the same things! They know they have needs and won't settle for less. But in some cases, they're not even aware of their wants. Customers don't require their wants be met to patronize your company, but if you do meet their wants, they'll be loyal."

"Give me an example," I said.

"Our coffee selection," I said. "Our customers expect our coffee to be hot and fresh. That's a need. But even a good gas station store can provide hot, fresh coffee. We give them a choice of exotic, flavorful varieties, with a million options. 'Double low-fat cap.' You ever hear that at a gas station? And if we serve it, and others don't, the customers are coming to us. Once they had all these choices, people discovered they're very particular about their coffee—a want they didn't know they had until we offered to satisfy it!"

"That's fantastic!" I said. I'd forgotten what it felt like to be challenged by an excited, innovative thinker. This is what I needed when I started my day!

"But, in fairness," Joe said, "you have to do more than just ask the customer. You have to capture customer needs and desires and translate them into actionable design requirements. In DFSS, it's called Quality Function Deployment, or QFD, and it's a tool for linking the objectives of marketing and designing—in other words, converting customer wants into specific corporate goals so that product and process designers know what to do to satisfy the customer. As one of my buddies called it, QFD stands for 'Quit Fooling with the Design, listen to your customers!'"

"Any chance you can give me . . ."

"An example?" Joe grinned, pleased with his anticipation. "Sure. Suppose you're planning a Hawaiian vacation for the family, and you call the hotel to make arrangements. What do you ask for?"

"Oh, I don't know," I said. "I'd make sure they have a room for the dates I want, for starters, at a reasonable rate, and preferably nonsmoking."

"Okay," Joe said. "Makes sense. What else?"

"Well, if it's a vacation in Hawaii," I ruminated, "I'd probably ask if I could get a room with an ocean view, the higher up the better."

"Good," Joe said. "Keep going."

"And I might also ask for more mundane things like airport shuttle service, exercise facilities, and a good restaurant on the hotel property."

"That's a good list," Joe said. "Now, suppose the hotel staff on the phone tells you that the hotel can meet all the requirements you listed—every one of them except the room rate, which is $500 a night. You the customer want a LOW room rate, and their room rate is HIGH. How do you feel?"

"Disappointed, for sure," I said.

"And rightly so," Joe said. "They didn't fulfill one of your Basic Needs. But suppose the hotel staff tells you that you can have all your preferences for 20 bucks a night."

"With everything I wanted?"

"Yes," Joe assured me.

"I'd be thrilled, of course," I said. "Are you kidding?"

"Alright, that's an example of advancing from having your Basic Performance Needs met to being delighted. Now, let's go the other direction: Let's say you take your family there. As you get into your hotel room and start unpacking, one of your kids comes out of the bathroom and says, 'There's no toilet paper in the bathroom!' How would you feel?"

"A little outraged," I admitted. "That's the kind of thing that would get me on the phone to the front desk immediately."

"Sure it would," Joe said. "Having toilet paper in the bathroom is something you wouldn't even have thought to ask for—Who doesn't take that for granted?—but if you don't have such obvious needs met, you'd be extremely dissatisfied.

"On the other hand," Joe continued, "suppose your kid comes out of the bathroom and says, 'There are six rolls of toilet paper in the bathroom.' Would you jump up and down and tell your spouse, 'We've just found the perfect souvenir for your mother!'?"

We both cracked up.

"No, I'm guessing not," I said.

"No, probably not," Joe agreed. "You'd have to say that having toilet paper in the bathroom is a Basic Need that goes unnoticed unless it goes unmet. Now, suppose you check into your hotel room and find an umbrella hanging inside the closet with a note that says: 'The staff of the Hotel Hawaii hope to anticipate everything we can to make your stay more pleasant.' How would you feel? The last hotel didn't provide an umbrella, and you most likely weren't even aware that such a service even existed, so you felt nothing about its absence. But once you discover the umbrella in this hotel room, you've experienced an Excitement Need, not something you require to satisfy you, but something that's needed to thrill you."

"I see your point," I said. "So put all this back together for me. What's the upshot?"

"The point is this," Joe said. "Basic Needs and Excitement Needs may be at the opposite ends of the spectrum, but they have something in common. Usually, they're both unspoken needs. Think of toilet paper on the one hand and an umbrella in your room on the other. You'd never ask for either one when you check into a hotel. So the lesson is this: If you only do what the customers tell you to do, you not only won't excite them, you might not even meet their basic needs."

"Hmmm," I said. "Interesting."

"In our case," Joe said, "the customers would never dare ask for free bottled water, but we give it to them, every time, with any purchase. Trust me, they notice!"

"I sure did," I admitted.

"Well then," Joe said, "now you've got it. You can see that Basic Needs merely get your company into the market and allow you to compete, while stepping up to satisfy the customer's Excitement Needs will gain your company a leadership position in the marketplace. DFSS gives us specific strategies to help define the spoken and unspoken needs of the customer, especially for Excitement Needs that typically represent future and unknown needs. We can get to these by letting the customer modify our product or service, or through lateral benchmarking, where we 'steal' ideas from the best in the business."

"Hmmm," I say, really thinking now. "Show me how."

DEVELOP CONCEPTS

"So, where are we?" Joe asked.

"Well, we've Identified and Defined the Opportunity."

"In this case, cutting down the customer wait time in line during the morning rush," Joe said.

"Right. And we've done it by finding out what the customer wanted."

"That's it," Joe said. "I'll tell you something: sometimes asking the customer can actually get you off the hook."

"What do you mean?" I asked. "By showing you the way, taking some of the responsibility off you?"

"Well, yes," Joe said. "That's true in every case, that customers can lead the way and take some of the burden off you to make all the decisions, to set all the standards. But what I'm talking about is, sometimes they'll actually tell you that some things you thought meant so much to them, really don't."

"Example?" I asked.

"Look at the cup in your hand," Joe said, and I did. "What color is it?"

"Brown," I said. "Beige. The color of cardboard."

"Right," Joe said. "And when we were picking everything we wanted for our store, we assumed that our customers would want smooth white cardboard cups—for cleanliness and purity. But when we asked them, it turns out that didn't matter nearly as much to them as the fact that bleached cardboard is an environmental problem—more toxins released into the environment to make them and harder to recycle. Today's customers, you know, have different values. So we put aside what we thought they wanted and gave them what they told us they wanted: unbleached cardboard cups. These cups were cheaper, too, it turns out, but that wasn't the point. Our customers are happier, and so's the environment."

"Hmmm," I said. "Lesson learned. So, after you capture the Voice of the Customer, what's next?"

"You make the darn brown cups!" Joe joked. "Or, to put it another way: you develop the concepts you need to give the customers what they want."

"And how do we do that?"

Brainstorming

"This is the fun part," Joe said, rubbing his hands together in a mockingly sinister way. "If you want creative concepts to please the customer, you have to think creatively, and work creatively. Obviously, there are as many ways to do that as you can imagine, but we can discuss a few of my favorites now. If you want more of them explained in greater detail, there are books for that, as I've said."

"So whatcha got?" I asked, now very curious what Joe had up his sleeve.

"We've got brainstorming, a related process called brainwriting, assumption busting, and something called TRIZ, among others. My favorite, though, is brainstorming."

"I know the general concept," I said, "where you simply bounce ideas around until one sticks."

"That's how it works in DFSS, too," Joe said. "Ironically enough, though, we actually *add* more rules to promote greater creativity. Sounds counterintuitive, I know, but it works."

"Try me."

"Brainstorming is a highly effective, though usually misunderstood, method for generating a lot of ideas quickly. The basic notion, as you know, is to get a few people sitting around a table, pick a question, and create as many ideas for solving it as possible. But there are several keys to doing it well, which if you ignore, reduce the whole thing to a sluggish bull session."

"Such as?"

"There are no bad ideas in brainstorming."

"Surely you jest," I said.

Joe laughed. "I'm not saying you won't hear some bad ideas—hopefully, lots of them!—but if people feel they're going to be judged by what they blurt out, they'll quit blurting things out, and you'll lose your creative edge. The goal is to open up the creative floodgates and let it all hang out, as we used to say. This way you get past the obvious, 'safe' ideas and discover the bolder, more innovative gems beneath them."

Joe probably sensed that I was halfway there, so he continued.

"Let's say you're coaching a basketball team," Joe said. "You would never put a player in the game, say good luck, and then add, 'Oh, by the way, one missed shot and you're out!' The kid wouldn't have a chance. He'd miss his first shot. You can't succeed if you're too afraid of failure. So, when you launch this brainstorming exercise, the rule is: ANY answer is a good answer. This is not *Family Feud,* where everyone responds to each other's answers, even if they are good.

"The most important goal in brainstorming is QUANTITY, not QUALITY. Don't worry: you'll be surprised how many good answers you get! You'll also be surprised how often a silly idea generates three or four good ones following it."

"Just let it fly and don't look back," I said.

> *The most important goal in brainstorming is QUANTITY, not QUALITY.*

"Exactly," Joe said. "In fact, it helps if you set a target number for the total number of ideas you want to generate."

"You can pinpoint it that accurately?" I wondered.

"Oh yeah," Joe said. "And you'll get them, too. How many do you think we should ask for?"

"Depends on the problem, I suppose," I said.

"Actually, it doesn't!" Joe replied. "See, you're back into the old mind-set, where you sit down and think your way through the problem, trying to come up with sensible, logical solutions. You'll freeze up, doing it that way. It's like the old word-association game, where someone says a word and you say the first thing that pops into your head, no matter what it is. The idea is to get beyond your conscious mind into the more creative subconscious realm. So remember, we don't care how GOOD the answers are, just HOW MANY! So, how many solutions do you want?"

"I don't know," I said. "Ten, maybe?" Joe didn't respond, so I reached a little higher. "Fifteen? Twenty?"

"Try 30," Joe said, "just for starters. It may seem impossible at first, but trust me, once people get going, they'll easily surpass 30. The high goal also encourages them to work fast and not think too much. Again, ANY idea is a good one, and it doesn't matter if it's silly, redundant, or impractical. Just let the wheels turn! It's even better if you have more than one team going at it to create a little competition among friends.

"Now," Joe asked, "how much time do you think we'll need to come up with 30 solutions, no matter how bad?"

"Oh, jeez," I said, feeling almost uncomfortable, because I was still trying to be realistic and calculate a fair deadline, when I knew that would be far longer than Joe wanted. "I don't know—ten minutes?" Again, Joe didn't flinch. "Okay, five?" I offered, though in my heart I knew that would be impossible.

"Would you believe three?" Joe asked, and put up three fingers.

"Three minutes, for 30 ideas?" I said, incredulous.

"Believe it or not, the shorter the time limit, the better. You'll usually generate 50 or 60 ideas in that short period of time. It's like preparing your tax returns: if you had no deadline, it'd take forever. Three minutes forces the team to MOVE, and in so doing, remove a lot of the mental blocks to generating creative solutions. It actually helps, not hurts, to have such a short deadline. The team members know they can't think rationally and finish on time. Panic is good, in this case!"

I was surprised to find myself laughing. Joe's enthusiasm and hell-bent approach had captured my imagination. I wanted more.

"Now, right before they begin, ask them to pick a 'recording secretary' at their table to write down the ideas. Number the page 1 to 30 and tell them they have three minutes to come up with 30 ideas, you don't care how bad. Thirty idiotic ideas are perfect. Thirty stolen ideas, fine. But 29 Nobel Prize–winning answers are sheer failure. You have to go to extremes to get them out of their normal way of thinking. As always, make your directions clear and direct. To keep things loose and show how the process works, you might consider giving them a sample subject first, like coming up with possible uses for a rake handle. In fact, let's see if we can come up with 30 ideas right now in three minutes. You ready?"

"Sure," I said, and turned to a clean page in my notebook.

"Ready . . . go!"

We ripped through the list. It was a blast! We flew out of the gate, coming up with so many ideas, so fast, that my pen could barely keep up—a lock for a sliding glass door, a baseball bat for street ball, a stick for growing tomatoes in the backyard, a limbo stick, even a rake handle! Whenever we stalled, Joe would throw out some silly suggestion like "attitude adjuster" or "giant toothpick." These obviously added a few more answers to our list, but more important, they loosened us up again to come up with more good ideas.

"Time's up!" Joe said. "How many do we have?"

I added them up. "Forty-two!" I exclaimed, stunned.

"Alright," Joe said. "Are you happily surprised?"

"Very much so," I said. "I really thought there was no way we could do it."

"If we had a couple more people, we would have gotten 60," he asserted. "But you're convinced that a lot of our answers are idiotic, aren't you?"

I laughed. "Guilty as charged."

"Okay, without looking, estimate how many out of 42 are useless?"

"Hmmm," I pondered. "Maybe half?"

"Well, let's take a look," he said. "Scratch off every dumb answer we had and see how many are left."

I went over the list, scratching off the silly ones I already mentioned, plus javelin, hockey stick, and Q-Tip for Mount Rushmore. But that was about it.

"Okay, how many dumb ones out of 42?"

"Only six, really," I admitted.

"And look, after each dumb idea, we had a flurry of good ones, until we stalled again and one of us said something silly to restart the process."

"You're right," I said, gazing at the pattern on my paper.

"So that leaves 36 viable ideas in just three minutes, including kindling, grill stirrer, and doggie fetch stick (if chopped up), and paint roller handle. Amazingly, we didn't come up with rake handle—what it's meant for!—until after we hit 30! So, what'd you learn?"

"I have to admit," I said, "we never would have been this creative or this productive or worked this fast without brainstorming."

"Bingo!" Joe said. "The brain works in funny ways. The time limit, the pressure, the crazy atmosphere— these all help us think 'outside of the box' better than any workshop, in my opinion. Now, after you do this sample exercise, you can give them the problem you really want to solve, be it fixing a persistent jam in the photocopier or solving the morning rush at a car dealership service department, and then let it fly!"

"This really works?"

> **A**fter you do this sample exercise, you can give them the problem you really want to solve, be it fixing a persistent jam in the photocopier or solving the morning rush at a car dealership service department, and then let it fly!

"Man, what do I have to do to convince you?" Joe joked. "Here, maybe someone else can get this through your thick head! Sandra?"

"Whatcha need, boss man?" she asked.

"Remember the brainstorming exercise?"

"Of course," she said. "I still think the Q-Tip for Mount Rushmore is a great idea."

"That was yours?" Joe asked, smiling.

"Oh yeah," she said. "But so was glass door lock, so I contributed."

"Remember what else we used brainstorming for?" Joe asked.

"Sure," she said, "just about every problem we've faced. The white paper cup question. Morning rush hour. The water dilemma."

"And did it work?"

"Better than any of us would've guessed," she said. "And it was fun. Painless, even! And quick—jeez! I think just about every good concept we've pursued here came from brainstorming. Using brown cardboard cups. Hiring more people for morning rush and cross-training them. Buying our own water spring— who would've dared say something that outrageous at a normal meeting?"

Joe looked at me. "NOW are you convinced?" he asked.

"Uncle!" I said. "You win!"

"Thanks, Sandra," Joe said.

"Any time," she said, and was off.

"For variety, or to solve even stickier problems, there are a lot of variations on this method," Joe explained. "The ones we've used here are channel brainstorming, analogy brainstorming, antisolution brainstorming, brainwriting, and assumption busting. They all have their benefits, and as you might guess . . ."

"I can read about them in the book back at your office, *DFSS*!"

"Bingo!" Joe said. "All brainstorming plays on the same techniques: teamwork, pressure, silliness—anything to get people thinking outside the box. Surprisingly, human creativity increases with certain limits, like time and quantity parameters, provided you're willing to let another standard go, in this case quality of ideas. Amazingly, you get quality ideas anyway! It's an old approach, really. The Jesuits called it, 'Freedom within Discipline.' Or, as General Patton liked to say, 'Don't tell them how to get there. Just tell them where they need to end up, and they'll find many more creative ways of getting there than you could ever think of.' And THAT is how you manage creativity!

"The point is," Joe continued, "relentlessly rational thinkers are valuable, but they don't change the world. Think of the 'old rules' that have bitten the dust throughout history, busted by people who were not afraid to question built-in assumptions. The world is flat, for one."

"The sun revolves around the earth," I offered.

"The people cannot govern themselves," Joe countered.

"Electricity can never be harnessed," I said.

"Man will never fly."

"Man will never walk on the moon," I added.

"Computers will never be small enough for personal use," Joe said.

"Packages cannot be delivered overnight," I said, closing out our list.

"Good thinking!" Joe said. "Clinging to the old way of thinking stopped everyone else from busting these assumptions, but not Columbus, Copernicus, Thomas Jefferson, Benjamin Franklin, the Wright Brothers, Neil Armstrong, Steven Jobs, and Fred

Smith, among others. That's why we remember their names and not the names of the thousands of people who said it couldn't be done, simply because it never happened.

"The key," Joe concluded, "is to create the kind of environment on your DFSS team that does not punish creativity, but rewards it. The first step toward doing so is never judging 'bad' ideas. You need not act on every idea, of course, but never scold anyone for coming up with potential solutions, no matter how far-fetched the ideas may be. You'll be surprised what can really work. Who would have thought customers would pay $3.50 for a cup of coffee in a brown cup?"

> *Never scold anyone for coming up with potential solutions, no matter how far-fetched the ideas may be.*

Sifting through the Solutions

"Okay," I said. "I can see you've got a lot of great ways to generate a ton of good ideas. But you can't pursue them all, so how do you pick the best?"

"That's the second goal in DFSS Phase II," Joe said, "to select the best solutions. The first step is to ferret out all the impractical concepts from the long list of possibilities, then narrow the list to just a few of the most promising prospects. If you can't get it down to two or three, you probably need to go back and redefine your goals. Then you've got to sift some more, combine the remaining ideas, determine what it would take to put them in motion, and follow up with a cost-benefit analysis, including risk. From there, it should be pretty easy to determine which solution concept to put in play for Phase III: Optimize Design."

"From the top?" I asked, anticipating Joe's next move.

"From the top!" he said, laughing. "The first step is called Screening for Acceptable Solutions. You do this by scratching off all those solutions that don't satisfy your 'non-negotiable' criteria—anything from legal requirements to safety issues to company policies.

"Take what's left, and then estimate each solution's likely benefit to the company against the estimate of the likely cost of the solution. The point is, even if a solution works, if it requires a very long 'run' for too short a 'slide,' it's not worth doing. When McDonald's had to face the environmental issues of its continued use of Styrofoam sandwich containers, it first tried to set up a recycling system to handle the problem. That quickly proved impractical, because the cost to separate the Styrofoam at the store and recycle it around the country proved far greater than simply switching to cardboard containers."

"I remember," I said. "So not every solution, even if it's ostensibly practical, is going to work."

"Exactly," Joe said. "I call this the 'triage' method of management, something Americans too often don't grasp. The question is not whether we should do this or not, but whether we should do this or find a better solution. Just because a solution will provide marginal help to the company, doesn't mean it's worth the time and effort. We want to get the maximum payoff for the minimum effort whenever we can. Look for the low-hanging fruit first."

"Example?" I asked, on cue.

"Of course," Joe said, grinning. "Take those cof-fee cups. We looked into different kinds of bleaches that would make the cups white but weren't as damaging to the environment. We also looked at new ways to recycle those bleaches, to avoid releasing harmful chemicals into the water. As we started looking into it, we realized the cost of undoing everything we'd done to make white cups wasn't worth it.

"Finally, one of our people said, 'The heck with it. Why not make brown cups?' And the cost savings were ridiculous. Half of the original cost! And they're so much better for the environment, too, without all those crazy extra steps. And the best part is, the brown cups have actually become a statement, a trademark of being earth-friendly. Our customers *prefer* them!

"So there you have it," Joe concluded. "A convenient example of sifting through the solutions for the easiest, cheapest, and most-effective one."

"Bravo," I said. "I get it."

"Thought you would," Joe said. "I should add that there are a lot of ways to sift through those candidates, which you can find . . ."

"In the *DFSS* book!"

"Yes!" We both laughed. "Regardless of which method you choose, it's a good idea to attack the process in two steps, by first narrowing down the list to the top few choices—creating the proverbial short list—and then 'war-gaming' the possible consequences of each individual choice, trying to determine possible outcomes. After that, a clear winner will emerge, and you're ready to move!"

TOWARDS PERFECTION

"This is where things get really exciting," Joe said, "because Phase III of DFSS, Optimizing the design, is where we shift from collecting information to making decisions using the information we have and taking action to create something special. We've got all our ingredients on the kitchen counter, so now it's time to start cooking."

"Good," I said, "I'm getting hungry."

"By now, we should know what our design goals are from listening to the customer, and we've picked a design concept that has a good chance of achieving those goals. We've Identified and Defined our goals, we've Developed a concept, so now we're going to Optimize that design—the 'O' in IDDOV. To me, this is the heart of DFSS. We're going to Optimize the design by using something called Robust Design® to determine the absolute best way to go about it, and then kick in Tolerance Design to figure out how to do it at the lowest cost without compromising quality."

"Tell me, I forget," I said, mimicking the famous Chinese proverb on learning.

"Show me, I remember," Joe followed, finishing the phrase. "Show you, I shall.

"A man named Dr. Genichi Taguchi created a two-step method to Optimize Design for Robustness, which goes like this: Minimize the variability, and then adjust the output to hit the target. In other words, let's first optimize the design performance, then adjust the outcome to make sure we've satisfied all the requirements."

"Sounds straightforward enough," I said. "And I like any process with only two steps!"

"Hear! Hear!" Joe said. "We start by determining the Ideal Function of the product or process. In the case of products, we try to make the transfer of energy in the system as smooth as possible. When we're making coffee, almost every ounce of energy should go into grinding the beans, heating the water, and pouring out a great cup of coffee, instead of getting wasted in a cloud of steam floating to the ceiling."

"Getting as much rubber to the road as possible," I said.

"Exactly. In the case of designing processes—like ordering food at our coffee counter—it's not energy but information that's transferred. Take invoicing, for example. The supplier sends us an invoice for filters, say, and that starts a chain of events that transforms the information into recordkeeping and finally a check being sent to the supplier. The smoother we do that, the better. The key to both designs is to minimize the variability, or the 'friction,' of that transfer."

"Got it," I said. "So how do we do that?"

Controlling Quality Control

"This is one of my favorite parts," Joe said. "To accomplish this smooth transfer, we need to rethink Quality Control. Since virtually the beginning of business, a 'good' product or exchange has been defined simply as anything that meets the standards we set. But there's a critical, though hidden, weakness in the old way of thinking: we've always assumed that ANY product or process that falls ANYWHERE in the 'acceptable' range is no better or worse than any other item in the same range."

"Like the old conveyer belt," I said, "where a line of apples roll along one by one, until they get to an inspector wearing goggles and a white coat, who inspects each one and dumps each into either the 'okay' barrel or the 'reject' bin."

"Perfect," Joe said. "In that factory, there are no other distinctions made among the finished products, just 'okay' or 'not okay.' Black or white—no shades of gray. Even though the inspector knows there are a million shades of quality in the apples he sees every day, he separates all of them into okay or not okay. But if you asked a typical apple eater if there was any difference between an apple that barely qualified as okay and one that was perfect, she'd say, 'Absolutely! You can easily tell the difference between the two.'"

> *There's a critical, though hidden, weakness in the old way of thinking: we've always assumed that ANY product or process that falls ANYWHERE in the "acceptable" range is no better or worse than any other item in the same range.*

"And, of course, the customer inspects them all herself and buys the better ones," I said.

"Naturally. To the customer, there's a world of difference between the merely acceptable apple and the excellent apple. Nobody just piles apples into their shopping basket, assuming that because they've all made it to the store, they're all the same. The point is: In the traditional approach to Quality Control, the company makes no distinctions among 'acceptable' outputs."

"But the consumer almost always does," I said, "so in this case, the company's out of step with the customer, it seems to me."

"'A' for understanding, my friend," Joe said. "You can easily see that the old way's not good enough in a highly competitive field. Instead of just barely meeting the lowest possible specifications, we need to hit the bull's-eye. And we're going to do that by replacing the oversimplified 'okay/not okay' bar with a more sophisticated bull's-eye design, where the goal is not merely to make acceptable products but to minimize the spread of darts around the target."

"What about the other side of the bar, the good side?" I asked. "You're replacing the over/under bar with shades of gray. But what about the top side?"

"Good question," Joe said. "We want to eliminate that, too. In the old system, once we met the specification, that's that—no point going past it. But in DFSS, even if we're already doing a good job on a particular task, we want to see if we can do it better—and if so, what would it cost us. Would improving it be worth it?"

"That's exactly my question," I protested. "Why should we bother making already good designs into great designs? After all, products don't give out 'extra credit' for exceeding the specifications."

"Oh?" Joe asked. "I think they do, sometimes. Let's take that apple again. If we can improve the harvesting process to ensure that the skin is never bruised, all of a sudden we have lots of chances to reduce real costs elsewhere. A better, more-resilient apple skin would allow us to use cheaper packing materials, to get rid of that wax used to cover up dark marks, and to save on labor, since grocers don't have to spend their time turning the apples this way and that to hide the blemishes. And if the cost of improving the skin is less than the cost of the better packing materials and labor, then we could save a ton *and* give the customer a better product."

"Actually, that sounds familiar," I said. "I just read an article about a company called Sampo that revolutionized the entire process of growing bean sprouts. Sprouts made from soy beans used to take seven days to grow into full-fledged bean sprouts, but Sampo found a way to reduce that to just four days. And not only that, their product tastes better, because the bean sprout cells are three days fresher."

"How'd they do it?" Joe asked.

"They took control of the things they CAN control, such as how often they watered the beans, what kind of minerals they added, and how much gas they mixed into the soy bean environment. The best part is, they did all of this without spending a cent more than the old way. Seven days was industry standard, and all Sampo competitors were happy once they reached the seven-day mark. The point is to not stop once you meet the requirements. In Sampo's case, improving from seven to four days without changing the basic design was the secret of Robust Design Optimization that encouraged it to go beyond the basic requirements towards achieving perfection."

"See?" Joe said. "That proves the point about optimization: You can improve a product or process without increasing costs through Robust Design Optimization. Typically, better performance does not mean it has to be more expensive."

"Ahhh," I said. "There's method to your madness!"

"Much!" Joe replied. "In our case, we decided to max out the quality of the coffee beans and water we use, which allowed us to spend less on filters and throw out batches of poor coffee. We almost never have to toss coffee out these days. And our employees don't have to be experts in judging coffee quality, either, because it's always there. It's built in."

> **Y**ou can improve a product or process without increasing costs through Robust Design Optimization.

"So you pay more for the beans," I said, "but less for everything else."

"Exactly. And you know, I've become convinced this notion of having 'no ceiling' is just as important for employee morale as it is for the bottom line."

"Give me an example!" I demanded.

"Let's take the IRS. Now the IRS, of course, tells you how much to pay, and virtually no one ever pays extra. Most taxpayers do their darndest to pay as little as legally possible. But charities never tell their donors what to pay—which might explain why Americans are by far the most-generous citizens around the world in terms of charitable giving, dwarfing the percentage of money other countries give. The point is, if you don't give your people an 'upper limit,' you'll be amazed how far past it they'll go. And when they do, you can use that improved performance to cut costs elsewhere. I can tell you—a limitless environment is a very inspiring place to work!"

"I bet," I said. And I realized, looking back on my day, that my old love for my work—that endeavor that takes up half our waking hours and so defines us as people—was coming back. I felt inspiration again, excitement, optimism to try new things. I could feel my well of enthusiasm filling up again. And, knowing that he'd have one, I couldn't resist asking Joe for another convenient example.

"An example?" Joe said. "Why did I know you'd be asking for that? Alright, let's look at the morning rush again. Now, at other coffee shops, what do you see?"

"A line, of course," I said.

"Of course. How long?"

"Oh, I don't know. Three or four deep?"

"Try seven," Joe said. "We studied it. It can get up to ten, easily. And, we also studied how many people walking up to the store saw the line, thought twice, and turned away. So, we decided to get serious about minimizing that problem and becoming a different kind of coffee shop."

"How'd you do it?"

"Well, first, we looked at the problem other stores were having," he said. "But, as you might expect, they didn't even see the long lines as a problem, but instead as a sign of good business! That was one big advantage we had, right off: the competition didn't care to shorten the lines. We discovered the reason they had long lines was simple: a few people behind the counter trying to do everything at once, with no specialization of skills. McDonald's figured that one out a long time ago—they've got a cashier, a fry guy, a burger guy—yet for some reason, coffee shops act like old general stores, taking ten minutes for the one person behind the counter to get everything you asked for. So, staff with specialized skills was one key."

"I'm with you," I said. "What else?"

"Another key was staffing," Joe continued. "Most coffee shops try to set the number of necessary employees by balancing their needs during rush hour with the downtime before lunch. So, they have too few during the rush and too many at ten, which basically means they're trying to minimize unnecessary staffing at both times by conceding that they're always going to have too few or too many."

"So how'd *you* solve this one?"

"First step," Joe said, "we didn't settle for four or five customers in line. We started out assuming the sky's the limit and then saw what real limitations we ran into, instead of creating self-imposed ones. Let's see who does it best—and try to beat them! You go to Vegas, don't you? What do you notice in the casinos?"

"No lines!" I said.

"Eureka!" Joe replied. "And why? They've ALWAYS got extra dealers, waitresses, and cashiers waiting for you, so you NEVER have to wait! And why should you have to wait to give the casino your money? Well, we figured we had the best and most-expensive coffee around, so why should we make people wait 5, 10, or even 20 minutes to give us $3.50 for it? For starters, we decided to make a policy of always having enough employees on hand to handle the customer load without having lines form. We figured that if each employee could serve at least four cups of coffee per hour, they'd more than pay for their own wages, including benefits."

"Good thinking," I said. "And pretty bold thinking, too, I might add. But what do you do with all the extra employees at ten o'clock?"

"Look around," he said with a grin. "How many employees do you see standing around chitchatting?"

I looked. I saw a half-dozen employees, all happily working. Not stressed, but busy.

"Now," Joe added, "how many employees do you see total?"

"Five or six," I said.

"Yet, we have 12 on staff at a store of this size at all times to handle the morning and lunch rushes. The others are in the back preparing the food, setting up the stations for fast, easy service when the time comes, ordering supplies, and working on our books. To avoid having too many employees or too few, the answer was *cross-training*. We set up our staff so everyone could do everything behind AND in front of the counter. That way, we can switch from giving one-on-one service to a specialized team approach when it gets crowded."

"The difference between man-to-man and a zone defense!" I said.

"Exactly!" Joe said. "The upshot? After we added staff, trained them, and cross-trained them, we discovered that we could provide customers great service with virtually NO waiting at ANY time! Now, that far exceeded our expectations—but that's what you can do when you don't settle for an 'upper limit.' With no waiting, we can bring in a lot more money per hour—customers will pay a lot for convenience, too, by the way—we do a better job keeping the customers happy, and we never have to skimp on bean quality. This shows you that exceeding one standard often allows you to worry less about another."

"Wow," I said. "I'm impressed!"

"We should talk about the flip side, though," Joe said. "If the optimum performance comes in *below* the requirements, it's time to rethink the design concept we selected in Phase II and come up with something better. The problem is, in most corporate cultures, that's a very difficult thing to do, because so many people would have spent so much time and effort on the project and would obviously be very reluctant to scrap it."

"How do you handle that hot potato?" I asked.

> *If* the optimum performance comes in **below** the requirements, it's time to rethink the design concept we selected in Phase II and come up with something better.

"In my opinion, this is where leadership comes in," Joe said. "Despite the heartbreak of letting an idea go, if it's not good enough, it's not good enough. Instead of spending good money on a doomed project and fighting the fires it creates for months and months afterward, it's best to cut your losses, reject the concept—salvaging the best ideas, if any—and move on to the next one. You've got to have the brains to detect poor designs and the guts to reject them at the earliest possible stages."

"How do you do that?" I asked. "Instinct?"

"To a degree," Joe said. "But DFSS never leaves anything to something so subjective. There is a tool for this, too, called Quality Loss Function, or QLF."

"Which I can find in the *DFSS* book?"

"Yes sir!"

Do Not Fight for Defects

"The goal of Optimization is simply to reduce imperfections like defects, vibrations, and poor reliability. To do that, we first have to separate these factors into those things we can control, like staffing, training, and stocking, and those we can't, like customer behavior, Mother Nature, and normal aging. If we do this right, we can make our entire operation—from the quality of our coffee to our service—less sensitive to, say, unexpected customer behaviors or unusually cold weather. We're looking to create smooth, pure outcomes, regardless of the factors we can't control. Today was an unusually busy day, but you don't see people rushing around here, do you?"

"No, I don't," I said. "I noticed that earlier. Always busy, never crazy. But every outfit has bumps in the road sometimes. How do you handle them?"

"I'll start by telling you what we DON'T do: ignore the bumps and hope no one notices, also known as the slip-it-under-the-rug response. Needless to say, this never solves the problem, but it's a surprisingly common response. We also decided to scrap the old trial-and-error method and not try to reduce the bugs after the fact."

"So what DO you do?" I asked.

"Robust Design," Joe said. "Instead of trial and error, which kicks in AFTER the 'noise' is discovered, Robust Design works to eliminate the effects of noise BEFORE it occurs. If you're going to go in this direction, you first have to get rid of your old notions of Quality Control—which really is a focus on failure—in favor of a new approach that focuses on SUCCESS."

"How so?" I asked.

"Well, instead of coming up with countless ways that a system might go wrong, analyzing those failures, and applying a countermeasure for each potential failure, we focus on how we can make things go RIGHT! It's a much smaller list, so it's faster to think that way—and much more rewarding, too."

> *Instead of trial and error, which kicks in AFTER the "noise" is discovered, Robust Design works to eliminate the effects of noise BEFORE it occurs.*

Joe then asked me to consider scientists versus engineers. It's the goal of scientists, Joe explained, to understand the entire universe, inside and out. A noble goal, surely, but not a very efficient one. It's the engineers' goal, however, simply to understand what they need to understand to make the product or process they're working on work better. For business, it's better to think like engineers, who look for solutions, and not like pure scientists, who look for explanations for everything under the sun.

"Our goal in DFSS," he said, "is to Optimize the product or process in a far more elegant fashion than just debugging or bolstering it would ever accomplish.

"Take our ordering process," Joe continued. "When you think about it, it's a nightmare to translate a customer's order, delivered orally, to a written order by the clerk, who passes it on to the person at the machine, who then reads the 'chicken scratch' to make the order. Right there, you've gone from speaking to writing to reading, from the customer to the clerk to the coffeemaker—a recipe for disaster. We could do it that way, but then we'd spend the rest of our day trying to make messed-up orders right for the customer.

"Instead, we have a process where the clerk is trained to repeat everything back to the customer as the clerk punches it into the computer register. This order comes up on a second screen that faces the customer, so they can see if we got their order right or not—right then and there. We can make corrections THERE, if necessary, before we make anything. Once the order checks out, the clerk simply pushes the 'send' button, which shoots the order in a uniform code to the coffeemaker—and voilà, a perfect order every time. And the best part is, you'd be amazed how often people will add to their orders once they see them on the screen. If you do it this way, you can duplicate perfection time and time again, no matter who the customer is, what they're ordering, or who's taking their order."

"It's variable proof!" I said.

"That's it!" Joe said.

Maximizing the Return on Investment

"Now, the next step," Joe said, "is to maximize the return on investment, which in DFSS is called Tolerance Design. Here's where we optimize our tolerances for maximum effect, which does NOT necessarily mean making them all as tight as they can be. Only a stupid race car driver tries to hug the inside curb all the way around the track. What it DOES mean is making them tight where they need to be tight, and loose where we can afford to make them loose. So we drive tight around the corner at the ideal point, then let our car fly to the outside of the track to maximize speed. That's how we get quality, efficiency, and thrift baked into our design."

"I'm with you," I said. I'm not a big race car fan, but I'd noticed how they used the whole track, just like Joe was saying, not just the inside of the lane. They drove down to the inside right in the middle of the turn, then let the momentum carry them almost to the outside wall just afterward, whipped to the outside like someone in an inner tube following a boat into a turn. There must be a reason for that, and the reason had to be speed. Who'd have thought the fastest way around the track was not the shortest distance?

"How about a . . . ?"

"Coffee example?" We both laughed. "When we were surveying customers, we learned they think it's imperative that our employees have bleached-white collars, because customers notice those and make judgments about our store accordingly. But, we don't need perfectly clean aprons. They need to start the day clean and be cleaned after every shift, but during the shift the customers expect us to have a little flour or sugar on our green aprons, because that means we're working to help them. So, we've learned to be very tight on collar standards—and a little looser about aprons."

"Good one," I said. "How about another example? I always prefer practice to theory."

"Thought so!" Joe said. "Here goes: Think of your list of specification tolerances as a baseball team's batting order, and you're the manager. Your job is to maximize run production, and you do it by trying different players in different spots in the lineup. The key is isolating who helps and who doesn't. Substituting various players in the lineup and changing the order will give you the results you need to determine who works best and where."

"Making the most of what you've got," I said.

"Exactly," Joe replied. "Remember Billy Martin?"

"Sure," I said. "Baseball manager. A little on the wild side, probably not easy for the owners to handle, but smart. Very smart."

"That's him," Joe said. "No question, he had his own off-field problems, but as a field general, he had no equal. One of the reasons he was so good was because he was smart enough first to see what kind of team he had, and THEN find a way to win with them. He played to their strengths and covered their weaknesses, unlike most coaches who have only one approach and, therefore, sometimes mesh with their players and other times don't.

"In the '70s, when Martin was managing the Detroit Tigers, a big but slow team, he emphasized power—extra base hits and home runs. When he coached the Oakland A's a decade later, however, he realized that team could never match Detroit's home-run power, but they were fast, so he switched his emphasis from big hits to base stealing, bunting, and hitting singles. In both places, he won division crowns, but with very different teams."

"Now THAT," I said, "is managing!"

"Yooouu got it!" Joe said. "The same principles work with DFSS Tolerance Design. We don't impose on the product or process what we THINK should happen. We look at what we have, surmise what improvements will get the best results, and test our theories. In Detroit, Martin didn't bother trying to make his team faster or steal more bases, because it wouldn't have worked. He made them focus on hitting even more home runs, and they did. In Oakland, he didn't make them lift weights and try to hit more homers, because they didn't have that ability. He made them get leaner and meaner and faster—and steal even more bases. And that's why it worked: he played to his teams' strengths.

"Now," Joe continued, "how do you apply this to DFSS? In a nutshell, you want to reduce costs by taking advantage of the tolerances that will improve your product the most with the least impact on costs. Tolerance Design is all about balancing COST against PERFORMANCE and QUALITY. When we changed our entire ordering system, we discovered that we saved a ton of money on reorders and also increased the speed of delivery to the customer—but it cost us more for better computers. Still, the balance paid off for us, or else we wouldn't be doing it."

> **W**e don't impose on the product or process what we THINK should happen. We look at what we have, surmise what improvements will get the best results, and test our theories.

THE FINAL TASK

The morning lull was giving way to the lunch rush—it was a little past 11 o'clock now—but just as Joe had told me, there really was no rush at all. Oh, the people were coming in and tables filling up, but there were no lines, and no one was frantic. Business was running like a well-oiled machine shifting from prep work to customer service, with everyone seamlessly slipping into his or her other duties.

"Okay," I said, wanting to make sure I had a handle on the process thus far, "in Phase I, we Identified and Defined our Opportunities for improvements, captured the Voice of the Customer, and came up with a rough draft for success.

"In Phase II," I continued, "we considered several Design Concepts and settled on the most appealing one—and by the way, I can't wait to try the brain-storming on my people! They're going to love it.

"And then in Phase III," I added, "we Optimized our Design Performance through Robust Design. So there's the three phases. What does that leave? Is our work done?"

"Almost," Joe said. "Remember, it's IDDOV—and we need a 'V' in there!"

"Gimme a 'V'!" I joked.

"You got it. The last step is Phase IV, in which we're going to Verify the optimized design by con-firming that it's working as we'd hoped it would. We'll do that by cementing all our work, so that it's not lost after the first project is completed. It's a busy step, but I think it's also one of the most rewarding, because we get to see the puzzle come together and begin to reap the fruits of our efforts."

"It's dessert," I said.

"Nice way to think of it!" Joe said. "And in many ways, you're right. We've got some work to do, for sure, but it's a lot of fun, too. A few rules of thumb apply here. One of the pillars of DFSS is our emphasis on baking quality into the design, not trying to squeeze it back into the mix after it comes out of the oven through trial-and-error methods. And that's why our designs have to be finished *before* we Verify them, instead of using verification as just another way to *revise* the design. In DFSS, we don't merely tack on as much quality as we can afford to after the fact. We design quality into the recipe from the start, and build the rest of the product or process around it. We need to let excellence, and not the calendar, rule the process, so we can avoid all the expensive, ineffective, and time-consuming fire fighting after the fact."

"And now, of course," I said, "it's time for the $64,000 question: How do we do all that? How do we Verify that we've done our job right?"

"Good news," Joe said. "Everything we need to do in this step was established in the previous steps, when we determined which *requirements* were essential to our design. In this final step, we simply take

> **O**ne of the pillars of DFSS is our emphasis on baking quality into the design, not trying to squeeze it back into the mix after it comes out of the oven through trial-and-error methods.

those requirements to Verify that what we've come up with will indeed satisfy our original intent. There are a lot of ways to do this, of course, which you can find out about—in the *DFSS* book!"

"Right!"

"So . . ." I said, rolling my hand over.

"Let me guess," Joe said. "You want an example."

"Bingo!"

"How'd I know that was coming?" Joe said. "If we were building a car, say, we'd build several prototypes for testing. First, we'd see how those models performed during one month of hard driving and try to determine what made some perform better than others. Then we'd give 'em the old *test to failure* to see how long they could maintain our standards before failing. After this step, we'd look at those models that could maintain the standards the longest and those that couldn't. Finally, we'd look to see which prototypes have the best combination of *stamina and quality,* and why."

"So now we've separated the men from the boys," I said. "What next?"

"We get our prototype together and put it through the Pilot Production Run, to find out if we can make these dream machines a reality or not. If we can't produce a successful batch of products or services, we know we're going to have big problems downstream if we don't fix it now."

"Basically, then, you're trying to see if the prototype is practical and repeatable," I said.

"Precisely. And this brings us to Process Control, one of the last stages of our work in DFSS. The whole point of the final phase, again, is to nail down our work, so we can repeat it again and again. There's no point in going to all the trouble to reinvent the wheel, only to lose the blueprints. That's why we record our work at every step of DFSS, so when we come up with the winning formula, we can make it again. And even better—so those who come after us can make it, too.

> **T**here's no point in going to all the trouble to reinvent the wheel, only to lose the blueprints. That's why we record our work at every step of DFSS.

"We might consider Process Control our own customized constitution," Joe added. "Our forefathers did incredibly heroic and noble work to earn our freedom, but unless they had recorded their new system in writing, we would never be able to follow it for future generations. It's amazing how well that blueprint works today—and how carefully we refer to it. In order to maintain their gains, they had to create a system that could duplicate their ideas of freedom and justice hundreds of years afterwards. For them it was the Constitution. For us, it's the DFSS Process Control Plan."

"Sounds like a recipe," I said. "Instead of just coming up with a great dish on instinct and savvy, you want to write it down so you or your kids can make it again. And you need to do it well enough that someone who's never met you can duplicate the dish to perfection."

"Exactly," Joe said. "And just like with a recipe, how detailed your directions need to be depends on how much risk is involved if the reader strays from it. Is it a dash of salt, or exactly one-eighth of a teaspoon? It depends on how much the salt affects what comes out of the oven. Another point: The more cooks who are going to be reading your recipe, the less you can take for granted. And that's ditto for employees when you're writing the Process Control Plan, because you don't know who's going to be reading it."

"Happened to me last week," I said. "I got directions to go to a friend's cottage, but my secretary wrote them down, and because she doesn't know my friend or the place, a few things got left out."

"You've got the idea. The more involved the translation, the more detail you need. When your buddy gave you directions, you didn't need a detailed account of every square foot of road, but you did need to know the crucial signs and details that would take you there. In DFSS, we need to determine the vital telltale signs that will most effectively guide future workers to success. And that's a skill as much as an art."

"If my memory of history class is accurate," I said, "perhaps the most ingenious aspect of the Consti- tution is that it includes ways to adapt and update it. I'm talking about adding amendments and the like. What about your Process Control Plan? If unforeseen changes take place down the road—and they always do—shouldn't we adapt and improvise the Process Control Plan, too?"

"Exactly!" Joe said. "The recipe that works for today's customer preferences may become outdated if the customers change their minds and want something else—and naturally they always do. The good news is that if we've taken the time and effort to complete the Process Control Plan, so every step is documented, we can refine them easily, as needed— just like the constitutional amendments you just mentioned."

Writing the Recipe Down

"One of the great things about this process," Joe continued, "is that the mere act of sitting down together to write it all down forces us to think it through a little more thoroughly. As they say, you don't know what you're trying to say until after you've already said it. Luckily, in writing, filmmaking, and so on, you can return to it, revise it, and improve it before the audience sees it."

"Example?" I chimed in.

"Coming right up! In this case, sitting down to produce our procedures manual will force us to consider what should be controlled, and by whom. The team's first thoughts on this topic will likely center around *Inputs,* all the things we need to deliver the *Output* successfully. For instance, to eliminate the chaos of morning rush at American Coffee, we knew we needed at least 12 staffers, we needed everyone to be cross-trained, and we also needed enough supplies so that employees had plenty to do after the rush ended."

"Gotcha," I said. "Then what?"

"After Inputs comes the *Process,* where the focus of the Process Control rightly belongs. Now, in this business, just like every other one, there's no shortage of things we COULD control, but if we insisted on controlling all of them we'd drive everyone nuts. So, our challenge is to decide what to control and what to let go of."

"Sounds like another triage process," I said.

"You're catching on, my man! If we examined every little step, we'd undoubtedly overlook the ones that really matter. So, we've got to make some tough choices to keep our eyes on the prize.

"Now," Joe continued, "after we've addressed the Inputs and the Process, it's time to move on to the Output itself. In this case, the Output can be a product or a process we provide our customers, whether they're internal or external ones. As I'm sure you've gathered by now, one of the pillars of DFSS is this: If we take care of our work upstream, we don't have to worry too much about what flows from the river into the sea."

"I'll buy it," I said, "but get back to the recipe!"

"Alright, my good man," Joe said. "As you wish. If we experiment with the recipe enough times, we'll discover which ingredients—and how much of each—influence the taste and texture of the dish, and which ones don't. I think the most-effective approach to Process Control is to start with the end in mind—that is, exactly what kind of product or process we want to create—and work BACKWARDS to figure out how to create that outcome.

"In our case," Joe continued, "we imagined a morning rush that wasn't rushed, with no lines and no frantic customers or staff. Now, how could we achieve that? With the final goal in mind, working backwards to fill in the blanks wasn't that complicated—not easy, but not complicated. The ultimate goal was to eliminate as many of the special controls as possible by making the product or process error-proof."

"This, I need to hear!" I said, feeling skeptical again.

Error-Proofing

"Error-proofing," Joe said, "is one of the most-effective ways to eliminate these special controls. And, unlike all those special controls that you have to enforce again and again, error-proofing is a one-time cost."

"Why's that?" I asked.

> **U**nlike all those special controls that you have to enforce again and again, error-proofing is a one-time cost.

"Special controls cost time and money every time you run through the process, for the entire life of the production run—a sort of tax you have to pay every day your design is up and going. So, it follows that each time you find a way to eliminate one of those special controls, you pay for the removal once, but the change pays dividends every day thereafter. It's like the difference between buying a car and renting one. The one-time hit may be costly, but after that you're saving money."

"Okay, that part I get," I said. "But I'm still not sold on how error-proofing works. Seems impossible to me!"

"Not at all," Joe said. "In fact, everyday consumer products have lots of error-proofing designs in them, and they're easy to understand. The manufacturer's first challenge is to 'customer-proof' their work. This is why we have safety guards on circular saws, cars that won't start unless they're in park, and three-pronged electrical plugs."

"Sounds more like idiot-proofing than error-proofing," I said, and Joe chuckled.

"You've never spilled your coffee?" Joe asked, eyebrows raised.

"Me?" I said, sardonically. "Never!"

"Well, for our mortal customers, we make sure the temperature of the coffee never exceeds 94 degrees Celsius."

"You don't need a lawsuit, obviously!"

"True enough—and these days, ANYONE can file a lawsuit over even the slightest inconvenience. But there are other reasons, too. We don't want unhappy customers walking around with scalded tongues for one. Upgrading to the more precise machines costs a little more, but it only takes one multi-million-dollar lawsuit to make up for that. And, just as important, it's also safer for our employees. After all, even smart consumers and employees can use our products and machines in ways that screw up the product, the machine, the person, or all three. The trick is to apply these generic concepts of error-proofing to all our products and processes."

"And how have you done that?" I asked.

"Look at your coffee cup," Joe said. "We always include the corrugated cardboard 'huggies' around the middle, so your hand never gets burned or even hot. Because when your hand gets hot, you may drop the cup and then all hell breaks loose. The coffee cup lid is specially designed to allow for sipping while preventing spilling, and the amazingly consistent temperature guarantees your coffee will never be too hot or too cold."

"Juuust right, then, like Goldilocks's porridge," I said.

"Now you're on to it," Joe said. "The second step of error-proofing is to reduce or even eliminate as many of the high-risk steps as possible—to reduce the damage human error can have. And finally, try to make each task you decide to keep simpler and more natural to perform, which is really a softer form of error-proofing."

"For example?" I asked.

"I give you the self-serve gas station, an idea that seemed impossibly dangerous and ill-advised just three decades ago. Today, it is virtually error-proof. How'd they do it? Clear, simple instructions on the pump. A safety handle that shuts itself off when the tank is full. And, if you're silly enough to drive off with the nozzle still in your tank—like I did one busy day—the hose releases from the pump and shuts off automatically."

"That," I said, "is a very good example. Well done. I suppose if we can make pumping gas safe for the masses, anything is possible."

"Couldn't agree more," Joe said. "Almost any process can be made safer through color coding and visual controls. Driving a car is probably the most dangerous thing we do each day, but it's been made a lot safer because 'go' is always green and 'stop' is always red."

"And, now that I think of it," I said, jumping in, "every traffic sign has its own unique shape and color, so you know immediately if you're looking at a construction sign or a yield sign without even having to read it. You usually know what kind of sign it is when you see it from behind based on its shape alone."

"I'm afraid you might be a convert to error-proofing, my friend!"

"Oh no!" I joked. "I got sucked in again! Darn this DFSS, anyhow!"

"Well, it's no worse than the way you converted me on Six Sigma a few years ago," Joe said. "That was a hard sell!"

"True," I agreed, "but as they say, converts make the biggest believers."

Bottom Lines

"So is that it?" I asked, amazed at how quickly—and easily—we had covered so much ground.

"Almost," Joe said. "The final task of the DFSS program is to Capture the Lessons Learned, because if we don't, all the wisdom gained will be lost for the next team and the next project it pursues. It's tempting to move on without this step, because it almost seems like an afterthought. But, it'll be as valuable as the Rosetta stone to future DFSS team members."

"So what does Capture the Lessons Learned entail?"

"To break it down," Joe said, "we need to capture the lessons we've learned with each tool and method applied, and with each function and discipline. Do this well, and that information will provide the control system for future projects. It will also allow all these 'secrets' to be owned by the folks in charge, the top brass, which ensures that DFSS won't be pushed aside for some fad that will inevitably come down the pike in the future. If the executives feel that the idea is theirs, they'll protect it."

> *We need to capture the lessons we've learned with each tool and method applied, and with each function and discipline. That information will provide the control system for future projects.*

"Ownership is always important," I said. "But one thing we haven't talked too much about is all the training, promoting, and other personnel issues that have to be addressed to make all this work."

"That falls under the heading of People Quality Management," Joe said. "But, to quote an old friend of mine, that's another story, for another day."

"Anything else today, guys?" Sandra asked, noticing our cups were empty. "No rush, of course!"

Joe gestured towards me with an open hand. "No," I said. "No thanks, Sandra. I think I'm all set."

"Me, too," Joe said. "Thanks, Sandra."

"Yes, and thanks for all your help," I added. "From the excellent coffee to the expert consultation."

"My pleasure, guys," Sandra said. "It's easy to help when you believe in what you're doing."

"I've got this one," Joe said, sliding a few bills into the leather folder. "Lord knows, I owed you!"

"Well, I think you're making up for it in fine style," I said. "This DFSS is something else. It's not at all hard to imagine how it's going to change the way we do business at American Pizza."

And, I could have added, it wasn't hard to imagine how it was going to change how I felt each morning when I got up, excited once more to take on the day's challenges.

"I think you're as hooked on DFSS as I was on Six Sigma after our last lunch," Joe said. "But wasn't there something else you wanted to discuss, something about a career decision?"

"Hmmm?" I asked, then remembered that I had written out my resignation that morning. I panicked for a second, until I recalled that I had slipped it into the top drawer for further consideration. Thank God! Well, I felt miles away from that desperate document now. I had ideas again, energy, inspiration, and hope. "No," I said to Joe. "No, nothing else. Just thanks."

Tomorrow, I can tell already, will be a brand-new day.

ACKNOWLEDGMENTS

For the development and production of this book I feel a deep sense of gratitude to:

- My friend, John Bacon, for his enormous support and hard work from day one, for refining the manuscript with integrity and a sense of quality, and for his continuous help and belief in my work.

- My Dearborn Trade Publishing editor, Jean Iversen, for her professional competence and project leadership—and for her continuous challenge.

- My very special friend in the publishing business, Cynthia Zigmund, vice president and publisher at Dearborn Trade Publishing, for her belief in every one of my writing ventures from the first day I met her, and for her continuous encouragement.

- Everyone at Dearborn Trade Publishing for their hard work: Leslie Banks, Elizabeth Bacher,

Robin Bermel, Mindi Rowland, Kay Stanish, Sandy Thomas, Paul Mallon, and Jack Kiburz.

- All of my dear friends and colleagues in the business, especially everyone at ASI–American Supplier Institute for their continuous support.

I am also grateful to my parents, Sushil and Krishna Chowdhury, and to my in-laws, Ashim and Krishna Guha, for their constant demonstration of love. This book would never have become reality without the support of my lovely wife, Malini. Of course, the newest joy in our daily life comes from our little daughter, Anandi.

ABOUT THE AUTHOR

Subir Chowdhury is executive vice president at the ASI–American Supplier Institute, the world's premier consulting and training firm on Design for Six Sigma and Robust Engineering. Hailed by the *New York Times* as a "Leading Quality Expert," Chowdhury was also recognized by *Quality Progress* of the American Society for Quality as one of the "Voices of Quality in the 21st Century." A respected quality strategist, Chowdhury's clients include Global Fortune 100 companies as well as small organizations in both the private and public sectors. Author of nine books, Chowdhury's most recent international bestselling books include *The Power of Six Sigma, Design for Six Sigma, Management 21C: Someday We'll all manage This Way,* and *Organization 21C: Someday All Organizations Will Lead This Way.* His books have been translated into more than 15 languages. He is frequently cited in the national and international media.

Chowdhury has received numerous international awards for his leadership in quality management and major contributions to the automotive industry. He was honored by the Automotive Hall of Fame, and the Society of Automotive Engineers awarded him its most prestigious recognition, the Henry Ford II Distinguished Award for Excellence in automotive engineering. He also received the honorable U.S. Congressional Recognition. In May 2002, the Society of Manufacturing Engineers honored Chowdhury with its most prestigious international honor, the SME Gold Medal. In 1999–2000, Chowdhury served as chairman of the American Society for Quality's Automotive Division.

Chowdhury lives with his wife, Malini, and daughter, Anandi, in Novi, Michigan.